PRASE FOR *TH*
LEARNING ADVISOR

Embark on a journey of transformation with *The Trusted Learning Advisor*. This book is a treasure trove of strategies, tools, and insights to transition from a traditional L&D role to a trusted business partner. Let it guide you and your colleagues towards becoming change agents for learning, development, and business performance!
Elliott Masie, Chair, The MASIE Learning Foundation

Dr. Keating's groundbreaking work serves as a transformative compass for L&D professionals and academics alike, offering not only an update on the latest in learning science but also illuminating the path towards fostering trust and building impactful relationships.
Dr. Raghu Krishnamoorthy, Director, University of Pennsylvania's Chief Learning Officer Executive Doctoral Program

The story of talent development is being actively rewritten. HR and learning professionals need to rapidly rethink how they prepare the workforce and workplace to address the evolving complexity of work. To develop and grow a future-ready workforce, L&D must bring a strong perspective, a flexible and strategic approach, and an end-to-end mindset to developing talent. In this book, Dr. Keating presents an actionable approach to help reverse the malaise that many L&D organizations now find themselves in. He offers an approach that recognizes how we must become more connected to the business, more consistent in our solutions, and more credible as trusted advisors that enable the outcomes both the business and the workforce need in today's work environments.
Brandon Carson, Global Head of Learning, Starbucks

Steeped in practical wisdom, *The Trusted Learning Advisor* is a game-changer for every L&D professional. It urges you to redefine your role, align your strategies with the business objectives, and prove the value of learning interventions. Let this book be your guide in your journey from being a simple order-taker to an indispensable strategic partner.

Matthew Daniel, Senior Principal of Talent Strategist, Guild Education

WARNING: This book contains learning and development GOLD. This notion of being an order taker is a constant battle in the L&D world. Many of us struggle with this daily. Dr. Keating has so eloquently articulated practical insights and strategies that will allow any learning professional to navigate the important role of Trusted Learning Advisor. It is so important that those struggles don't become battles, but rather opportunities to build strong relationships with strategic partners. Once the key is turned, prepare to unlock excellence and the full potential of your learning programs!

Stephanie Curry, Manager, Cadillac Academy

The ability to learn, unlearn, and relearn has never been more critical for organizations in these challenging times. Dr. Keating's *The Trusted Learning Advisor* provides readers with practical wisdom, invaluable tools, and transformative strategies that equip L&D professionals with all the tools they need to lead their companies to become places where learning is a strategic advantage.

Paul Estes, VP, Magic Leap

For years, the HR function has been striving to transition to the role of trusted business advisors. All too often the Learning & Development function has forgotten that it is either directly part of the HR function or at least tangentially connected with the explicit goal of unleashing the capability of both individual employees and the collective organization. In his book, *The Trusted Learning Advisor*, Dr. Keith Keating aptly zeros in on this oft made mistake of L&D leaders and highlights proven practices that can help the most junior to the most senior L&D leaders become trusted advisors to the business. His book is a must-read for any L&D leader looking to bring true purpose to their role and impact to their organization.

Clint Kofford, Chief Talent Officer, Covetrus

There is a great change that needs to be made in the learning and development industry and leaders like Keith Keating, who have the authority, experience and clearly well researched practices to back it up, are going to be the ones to help strengthen the wave of momentum. *The Trusted Learning Advisor* provides a truth and sincerity that needs to be heard, while giving you tangible and practical strategies to evolve and be better integrated into the learning worlds of your organizations. Read it.

Lauren Waldman, Founder and Learning Scientist, Learning Pirate Inc.

Embrace the future of learning and development with The Trusted Learning Advisor. This captivating book offers L&D professionals a wealth of practical advice, tools, and strategies to elevate their role from order-taker to trusted strategic partner. By aligning learning strategies with business objectives and influencing key stakeholders, you'll become a driving force behind your organization's growth and transformation. Prepare to embark on a journey of personal and professional transformation with this invaluable guide.

Alison Redpath, Learning Leader, HSBC

An L&D champion and a Trusted Learning Advisor himself, Dr. Keith Keating now shares over 20 years of invaluable, hard-earned experience on navigating the challenging, day-to-day delivery of corporate L&D and performance improvement successfully. Leaving no stone unturned, he covers everything from managing stakeholder expectations right through to personal, continuous development and branding. A motivational and experienced mentor, Keith's optimism and positivity throughout is infectious. I highly recommend The Trusted Learning Advisor to anyone, from those only starting out in L&D, to those looking to reflect upon and improve their current practice.

Dr. Markus Bernhardt, Consultant, ChangeUp Operations

The role of the L&D professional must transform to meet stakeholder and shareholder demands. The Trusted Learning Advisor outlines this transformative pathway to ensure that the role L & D is no longer a transaction, but rather strategic partners with credibility and reliability. This is a must-read for any L&D professional!

Dr. Chris Bittinger, President, Open Pivot

The Trusted Learning Advisor effectively captures an approach that will allow learning practitioners to ensure they deliver real organizational value. Developing the skills to become an internal consultant that can genuinely move the needle is priceless and timeless.

Adam Stedham, CEO, GP Strategies

The Trusted Learning Advisor

The tools, techniques and skills you need to make L&D a business priority

Keith Keating

KoganPage

First published in Great Britain and the United States in 2023 by Kogan Page Limited

Apart from any fair dealing for the purposes of research or private study, or criticism or review, as permitted under the Copyright, Designs and Patents Act 1988, this publication may only be reproduced, stored or transmitted, in any form or by any means, with the prior permission in writing of the publishers, or in the case of reprographic reproduction in accordance with the terms and licences issued by the CLA. Enquiries concerning reproduction outside these terms should be sent to the publishers at the undermentioned addresses:

2nd Floor, 45 Gee Street
London
EC1V 3RS
United Kingdom
www.koganpage.com

8 W 38th Street, Suite 902
New York, NY 10018
USA

4737/23 Ansari Road
Daryaganj
New Delhi 110002
India

© Keith Keating 2023
The right of Keith Keating to be identified as the authors of this work has been asserted by him in accordance with the Copyright, Designs and Patents Act 1988.

ISBNs
Hardback   978 1 3986 1247 1
Paperback   978 1 3986 1245 7
Ebook   978 1 3986 1246 4

British Library Cataloguing-in-Publication Data
A CIP record for this book is available from the British Library.

Library of Congress Control Number
2023943903

Typeset by Hong Kong FIVE Workshop, Hong Kong
Print production managed by Jellyfish
Printed and bound by CPI Group (UK) Ltd, Croydon, CR0 4YY

Kogan Page books are printed on paper from sustainable forests.

CONTENTS

ABOUT THE AUTHOR

With a career spanning more than two decades in learning and talent development, Dr. Keith Keating is a Chief Learning & Talent Officer, having worked with numerous Fortune 500 companies where he utilizes learning sciences, or how people learn best and under which conditions, as a scientific method supporting the development and lifecycle of global talent.

An author as well as a practitioner, Dr. Keating wrote *The Trusted Learning Advisor* as a call-to-action manifesto for L&D practitioners to evolve from order takers to Trusted Learning Advisors. By following the practical insights and strategies outlined in the book, he believes L&D can live up to its full potential of creating value for organizations while positively impacting the lives of learners.

Dr. Keating is not only an advocate of the benefits of education and its power to lift and match talent with their higher goals, but also a scholar-practitioner, earning two master's degrees and a doctorate in organizational learning from the University of Pennsylvania.

A celebrated advocate for talent development, Dr. Keating leverages his platform to underline the value of human talent as the cornerstone of organizational success. Driven by a passion to encourage, enable, and empower talent, he champions lifelong learning as the key to seizing control of one's career trajectory.

FOREWORD

My entire career has been spent trying to encourage organizations to maximize human potential, innovation, and performance in the workplace. To successfully achieve this, we need quality Learning & Development (L&D) practitioners. However, for a long time, L&D practitioners have kept in the shadows, being led by the business with an occasional opportunity to provide consultative input or expertise. Dr. Keith Keating strongly advocates for a new set of L&D practitioners, an evolution that requires a transformational journey which he beautifully outlines in this book. He shows the reader what the necessary skills are, and proves that these are what organizations really need to become Trusted Learning Advisors.

I like this book! It does what it says it will do: chart an essential rite of passage for any self-respecting L&D practitioner. The book starts where they may start; in a place that is comfortable, subservient, and in the context we find ourselves, short-lived. The book drops us off in Chapter 10. By now we are in the sunny uplands of power, authority, and presence inside the organization. Keith shares the best of the best practices when we become what the book defines as "Trusted Learning Advisors."

The author does not see this trajectory as a series of choices to make or ignore; rather, these changes are fundamental and necessary: "Our need to evolve into Trusted Learning Advisors starts as self-preservation for our role within the workplace" (Chapter 3). This theme creates a sense of urgency for this change which runs solidly throughout the book. It is written with a passionate intensity and commitment. There are few downsides to this shift, in the eyes of the author!

Therefore, this book has its agenda. And so it should. Every example and mini case propels the reader to a singular vision: this change is necessary and inevitable if you want to survive amidst a period of intense disruption and uncertainty and provide meaningful impact for the organization.

The book tackles some fundamental issues inside L&D. The basic question which underlies the book asks whether L&D staff are practitioners or order takers. If we visit a physiotherapist, and we tell her that the seat of discomfort is here or there, she is trained to listen carefully and then after some investigation point out that the root cause is somewhere completely different!

She is a practitioner; she evolves her practice consciously and deliberately throughout her career. She has to be a life-long learner, who aligns with her colleagues, takes on new treatments, and absorbs research as a matter of course. Her license is predicated on keeping up with current practice, absorbing new ideas and the latest research as well as experimenting with new treatments. We would have no confidence in someone who listened to our complaints, took us at our word, and began treating us without further exploration. That is not what practitioners do! So why, according to the author, would L&D practitioners behave in such manner?

In L&D there is a battle to be respected and accepted as a practitioner and not treated as an order taker. If anyone takes their practice seriously, and behaves like a professional, they must be able to have serious conversations with stakeholders and challenge their assumptions in order to get at the root cause, not the symptom. But it takes both sides to align and agree that this is the right way to go forward for any regular or consistent partnership to occur. This book takes you on that journey to professionalism; it helps you have those conversations and feeds you with success cases.

The impact of this journey is not simply about better learning, more appropriate content, or more sophisticated measurement of impact. The book argues that this process gets to the heart of making meaningful work, building a better workplace, and increasing motivation. The net impact is huge, in performance and efficiency terms. So, this is beyond learning and beyond L&D. It is about the way an organization looks at itself and the way it treats its staff and accesses their ideas and creativity. An organization with learning at the heart of performance needs to have more than just a "showing up" culture.

There is a change that needs to happen for L&D, an institutional change, and it starts with changing our perspective and thinking of ourselves as Trusted Learning Advisors. You are taking the first step toward change by reading this book. Please take those insights and turn them into action.

At the heart of this book is an optimistic sense that we cannot just do learning better, but we can do work and work environment better. Who would not want to come along for that ride?

Nigel Paine

ACKNOWLEDGMENTS

They say it takes a village. In this instance, it took a tribe. Thank you to my tribe.

To Dr. Nigel Paine—thank you for your years of commitment to our industry and striving to make us all better practitioners. And thank you for writing the Foreword. I'm honored to have my name alongside yours.

To Cecil Abraham and Sean Stowers—thank you for your time to review this manuscript and provide valuable insight and feedback.

To Loren Sanders, Dr. KimArie Yowell, Dr. Clint Kofford, Britney Cole, Lauren Weinstein, Clark Quinn, Guy Wallace, and John Hagel—thank you for your important perspectives and for allowing me to include your experience in this book.

To Greg Cira—thank you for the time spent on the design (even if it wasn't able to be used).

To Adam Stedham—I haven't forgotten that you have helped push me toward being the practitioner I am today. Thank you.

And to my parents—thank you for encouraging me to write from a very young age. It only took 30 more years, but I'm finally getting there.

Introduction

"Those who do not move do not notice their chains."

ROSA LUXEMBURG

Progress requires change. It has never been clearer that those of us in the field of Learning & Development (L&D) are the changemakers for our organizations. We are an integral piece of the puzzle for achieving growth. For decades, we have sat by while others called the shots, made the decisions, and told us how, when, why, and what type of training or learning interventions we would use in our organizations.

Many of us are still there—comfortably nestled in the familiarity of playing the role of an order taker for our organization's L&D needs. Some of us even justify it by adopting the belief that we should stay in our lane and focus on the work we're being asked to do. But every great innovation in life begins when someone has the courage to ask, "but why?"

Why are the experts in learning letting someone else tell us when training is needed?

Why do we let them decide what, why, when, and how that learning occurs?

Why are we not consulted when big decisions are made?

Why are we trying to get a seat at someone else's table instead of inviting them to ours?

As humans, we are programmed to seek out what is familiar. From an evolutionary standpoint, we're even programmed to avoid anything that makes us uncomfortable. Once upon a time those signals of heightened alertness were designed to keep us alive. Today we use the unpleasant feeling of anxiety or fear as a convenient excuse to maintain the status quo.

And while "what we've always done" feels familiar and comfortable, there is no room for growth or improvement in complacency. As we head into the next evolution of the way work is accomplished in organizations, the opportunity for L&D to evolve within the organization is going to be pivotal in the ultimate success or failure in navigating the next phase of the digital transformation and talent development.

The future of work is automated, but it is also human. Technology will give us efficiency and access to information that will change the game for what is possible. But that innovation will be wasted if our human talent doesn't rise to the occasion and use these tools to be better. The digital and talent transformation necessary for success is entrenched in skilling, reskilling, and upskilling an entire workforce. It is a huge undertaking. And it belongs to L&D.

Now is our time to shine, but we can't do it from our comfortable silos. We need to be out in front, leading the way. Rather than fighting for a seat at someone else's table, we need to invite others to sit with us. L&D needs to become a trusted resource and advisor for leaders in the organization to turn to for effective analysis, problem solving, and practical solutions.

But alas—there is a big divide between knowing what we should do and effectively doing it. When L&D is treated like order takers or behaves like order takers, it circumvents the true power and value of learning from being recognized in the workplace. It limits the growth of the organization and talent inside. As Dr. Nigel Paine says in Chapter 3, the idea that L&D are still order takers is depressing. The need for L&D to step up, to stop being order takers and act like Trusted Learning Advisors has been ongoing for the last 20 years, but nothing has changed.

This book is the consent L&D needs to be empowered and change.

Since the inception of formalized workplace learning, managers have dictated how employees need to be trained. Up to today, L&D functions have been taking and executing orders by those outside of the field. Evolution is required for survival and L&D is no exception. The future of L&D workplace learning hinges on the L&D industry evolving into Trusted Learning Advisors. And it starts with you.

This book is dedicated to finding actionable ways that move the needle towards progress in developing a relationship with your stakeholders that positions you as a Trusted Learning Advisor.

"The only person you are destined to become is the person you decide to be."—Ralph Waldo Emerson

Who Is This Book For?

As an L&D practitioner, I believe we each have two paths before us. We can choose the familiar path that is safe and comfortable as order takers, or we can rise to the occasion and be the agents of change that our stakeholders, learners, and organizations need us to be—Trusted Learning Advisors.

This book is your permission, encouragement, and manifesto to be different than you have been for so long… to be better.

Anyone and everyone can be a Trusted Advisor. And while the principles in this book can largely apply to anyone, I wrote this book from the specific lens of and for those in the field of human development: L&D, human resources, talent development. L&D happens to be my passion, my life, my purpose, and in great need of this type of attention.

For entry-level practitioners who are considering a shift to the L&D industry or just starting their careers, I want to shape for you the aspirational goal that all L&D practitioners should have—to be a Trusted Learning Advisor. I want to share with you the practices, behaviors, skills, tactics, and strategic ways forward that no one ever shared with me, but which took years to cultivate. I want this book to serve as your "welcome guide" to this beautiful and complex industry, sharing with you the foundational information necessary to set you up for success. I want to dig into specific opportunities and experiences that you need to cultivate to grow and evolve. And as much as possible, I want to provide important context for these decisions. We are in the midst of big changes, and you are the future of our industry. Things are moving quickly, so to plan for your future, you need to be focused on changing *what hasn't worked for today* into *what will set us up for success tomorrow.*

For mid-level practitioners, you have been in the industry for some time and have probably experienced everything I've discussed in this book. You know the frustrations of being kept in a box, passively being given orders, and not being heard. You know that much of what you have been doing could be done differently or better, but you aren't sure how to change the situation you are in. I want to call attention to the current state of our industry and discuss a need and a way to change. I want to meet you where you are in your journey and provide strategic and tactical ways to begin developing the right relationships to achieve the status of Trusted Learning Advisor. I want to provide you a toolkit to be used today to change the course for your career and for your organization.

For senior-level practitioners, we have enabled the behaviors and beliefs that we are order takers long enough. We commiserate at our conferences, we write about it in our industry publications, and yet we haven't fought hard enough to change it. Understandably—as the experienced practitioner, it gets exhausting being told over and over what to do and how to do it by someone outside our field of expertise. Maybe the voice telling you "there is another way" has gone quiet or the spark of fire to drive change is now a soft ember. Maybe your purpose has been forgotten. Let this be the reminder, the call for change to start today to live up to your full potential and evolve from order takers into Trusted Learning Advisors. After being set in your ways for so long, you may face the most difficult challenges by already having established relationships and expectations based on your tenure—which also makes you the most pivotal role to drive this needed change.

You are not just changing your own behavior but the behavior of each individual person on the team you are leading. It's up to you to digest the philosophies and methodologies described here and then bring your team on the journey with you. This is a collective effort, requiring each one of us to develop the skills and behaviors necessary to be Trusted Learning Advisors. We are the experts in learning, and we need to use our expertise to shape the cultures within our organizations so that everyone is open and receptive to the idea of growth through learning.

Not only do we need to be actively involved in the conversations that matter, but we need to be leading the conversations so that we have opportunities to demonstrate our value. And we need to emerge as the leaders that guide our organizations through the process of building up a pool of agile human talent that will be prepared to pivot effortlessly as organizational needs change in the years to come.

My hope is to give all L&D practitioners, regardless of where you are in your career, the permission to be curious, to ask questions, and to do the due diligence necessary to understand the problem and the people being impacted. I want this book to provide inspiration for change regardless of where you are in the journey. I want to provide insight and a roadmap into the skills necessary to be treated with the same respect that the auto service technician, dentist, vet, computer tech, doctor, or any of the other skilled practitioners who are treated as Trusted Advisors receive. I want to empower our industry to achieve our highest purpose: changing lives through the power of learning and development.

If you're ready to take one step towards future-preparing your L&D career and evolving as practitioners, I invite you to read this book and start your journey to becoming "The Trusted Learning Advisor."

"Beware of unearned wisdom"—Carl Jung

My Story

Over 20 years ago I lucked into the field of L&D after answering an ad in the newspaper. I was a high school dropout with an understanding of Microsoft Office who found his way into training the government on their transition to Microsoft Office 2000. Although I had no business being in the room, according to my manager, my clean driving record and propensity for traveling to small towns said otherwise—neither reason speaking to my skillset as a trainer because none existed.

I had no idea what I was doing and probably caused more harm than good for the first six months of classes I taught. But I have perseverance, or as my vocal coach once told me (before encouraging me to stop wasting my money on her), I have tenacity. I wasn't a good trainer, but I was consciously aware I wasn't a good trainer. I knew if I practiced every night and didn't give up, I would get better. And I did. Eventually I saw the light come on in people's eyes when I was able to help them learn. For one of the first times that I could remember I felt a spark, I felt that I had a purpose, and it felt good.

Fast-forward two decades and I'm now a Chief Learning Officer (CLO) with a doctorate with distinctions in Organizational Learning from the University of Pennsylvania. I know both the challenges of a formalized education system and the power of unlocking the ability to learn—starting with my own.

Over the years I've learned the difficulty I had in school and my struggles with learning have become a superpower. Whereas the formal education system failed me in many ways, when I taught myself something in a way that I could understand, I was able to then convey that knowledge to others in a way that they easily understood. Maybe it's empathy for experiencing learning challenges myself or creating a safe space for myself to learn... whatever it was, I was a conduit to disseminate knowledge to others.

This book is a culmination of my 20+ years' experience, lessons learned, and behaviors cultivated allowing me to have the career I have today as a Trusted Learning Advisor. Today my stakeholders trust me. They listen to me. They join me at my table to talk about learning challenges, the future, and how L&D can solve for or at least help them prepare for tomorrow. This is a place of privilege, one that has taken years to achieve, and one that I hope many of you aspire to be in.

And you can.

But it isn't easy. It wasn't given to me—it was earned. And it isn't forever. There are still situations where stakeholders want me to be an order taker, but I work daily to maintain the status of Trusted Learning Advisor.

I have been exactly where you might be today—stuck, disillusioned, and even bored. I have been comfortable. I have been complacent. But I have been learning and growing. In comparison between the first decade of my career when I was blissfully ignorant of my role as an order taker and genuinely happy to be there and the last decade as I have grown to adopt a business-centric, learner-centric view with an eye for the future, I can confidently say that I love the growth and the powerful potential we have to drive impact and create value as L&D practitioners.

Michio Kaku once said, "Knowledge is useless if it's not shared." This book is me sharing with you everything I have learned to help you develop the skills and practices you need to transform into a Trusted Learning Advisor. As a Trusted Learning Advisor, my hope is that you will find the same spark and purpose I feel every day.

From Order Taker to Trusted Learning Advisor

01

"The person who follows the crowd will usually go no further than the crowd."

ALBERT EINSTEIN

Julia was a seasoned Learning & Development (L&D) practitioner with 12 years' experience across multiple industries. Having been with her previous company for several years as the manager of the learning department, she was ecstatic when she was recruited to a new company as the director of learning. Although she enjoyed her former company, she felt she had accomplished as much as she was able to within the given culture. Julia consistently felt she and her team were held back from delivering on their full impact and were treated like order takers. The recruiter and hiring manager assured her the new company had a culture of learning and, most importantly, learning had a seat at the table to drive change.

As do many new hires, Julia started energetic, hopeful, passionate, excited, and filled with ideas. She knew the importance of building relationships with her L&D team and her stakeholders and the importance of taking time to listen and understand before proposing ideas or changes, particularly as she was the newly hired learning leader. But it wasn't long into her listening quest before Julia spotted familiar red flags.

When outlining their current relationship with their stakeholders, Julia's new L&D team explained that their communication cadence with their stakeholders was reactive. "When I get a call or an email, it's usually last minute and urgent." The team also felt a disconnect and frustration existed with their stakeholders. "Even after executing what was asked, we get blamed when the program or the eLearning they asked us to create didn't have the outcome they wanted. But we did exactly what they asked, and it's somehow our fault."

Julia wondered whether the team had the skills necessary to conduct a needs analysis to identify the problem that the learning initiative was attempting to solve. The question was indirectly answered before it was asked. "Sometimes I'm not even sure what we are trying to fix," her team noted. "I feel like we spend our time reacting to what our stakeholders want... but it seems like reacting is all they want us to do." When asked if the team was embedded in the business, they curiously asked what she meant by that question. And when asked how they measured the value of their work, the team happily explained their after-class and eLearning surveys always showed they had great results.

This wasn't an unfamiliar story to Julia. She'd been a part of several learning teams that shared similar sentiments, having left her last one in hopes of advancing past learning being treated as or acting like order takers. Julia recognized she could influence and grow the behaviors and skillset of her team; this wasn't an area of concern. The stakeholders, however, would prove to be a different story.

"We appreciate that the training group does exactly what they are asked to do."

"The training team provides our training."

"The stuff is kind of boring, but it gets the job done most of the time."

Stakeholder after stakeholder repeated a similar story during Julia's initial stakeholder interviews. When asked how the stakeholders determine if a project is successful, two statements were consistently repeated: on time and on budget. No stakeholder talked about wanting to drive behavior changes through L&D or utilizing the learning team to drive business results.

Julia asked stakeholders about having more strategic learning discussions on a recurring basis and was met with a resounding "But why?" Realizing that there was no table where L&D had a seat like she'd been promised, her heart sank.

"Uh oh," Julia thought, "Here we go again."

The initial tone of the stakeholder conversations was a glimpse into their larger attitude toward the learning function. After several months of feeling the continued pervasive stakeholder resistance, Julia acquiesced back into the subservient mindset and behaviors she was trying to avoid by leaving her last organization. To Julia, it just seemed easier to fall in line with the stakeholder expectations; she didn't have the energy to lead in another direction.

Where Did Julia Go Wrong?

It wasn't just energy that Julia lacked (remember, she started with the energy); it was skills. Based on her experience, Julia knew the caution signs of stakeholders who were difficult and challenging, but she had not yet learned the art and skill of being a strategic partner rather than just a learning provider. Julia had not learned how to be a Trusted Learning Advisor.

I've been Julia—many times. I imagine you have been Julia before, or even feel like you are Julia today. But you have what Julia didn't have—these pages to help guide you on your transformational journey into becoming a strategic learning business partner, otherwise known as a Trusted Learning Advisor.

A Premonition

If you haven't already, sometime soon you will be faced with a stakeholder (business partner, line manager, executive, client, customer, or anyone with a stake in the work you are doing) who asks you to deliver a training program to fix what they perceive to be an urgent problem. Perhaps your stakeholder is alarmed because sales goals are being missed, there has been a rise in product defects, client satisfaction is on a downward trend, or their team appears unmotivated and prone to interpersonal conflict.

Your stakeholder, who is likely to be showing a hint of stress or even panic, wants a training program that does not take people away from work for long—perhaps something that would take an hour or two, a half day at most—to cauterize the issue and get the team back on the right track.

If you, as the L&D practitioner, simply listen and nod politely, ask how soon they need the program and then agree to deliver it to their specifications (like Julia's team), you are acting in the role of order taker.

The order taker lifecycle:

- Someone else identified the problem.
- Someone else identified the solution.
- Someone else told you what to do.
- And then you did it.

In these types of transactions, you aren't asked for your professional opinion about the potential performance issue nor about the type of learning intervention that might best address the perceived issue—or *if* a learning intervention is even appropriate in solving the problem. Instead, someone else already decided that a learning intervention would solve the problem, they provided no time or space for you to understand what problem the "order" is attempting to solve, and they want you to execute the request to magically make everything better.

But like most such dilemmas, the problem is not one-sided. For a number of different reasons, it's likely you, as the L&D practitioner, did little in this scenario to speak up and persuade your stakeholder to pause, catch their breath, and collaborate with you on looking deeper into the root cause of the performance problem before rushing headlong into executing the prescribed training solution.

Most likely, no one told you that being consultative, strategic, and collaborative was an option.

After all, there is a longstanding belief both in the business and in the L&D profession that you exist to serve the business and what the business wants, it gets, with few questions asked. It's not easy in such scenarios to risk upsetting those who write the proverbial check.

You have been conditioned to see your role as delivering exactly what the stakeholder requests in the fastest, most cost-effective, and highest-quality fashion possible, regardless of whether it's the right solution or will actually solve the problem.

So, what's the alternative?

Evolving into Trusted Learning Advisors.

What Is a Trusted Learning Advisor?

A Trusted Learning Advisor is an individual that works collaboratively with their stakeholder as a strategic consultative business partner. Leveraging extensive L&D experience and knowledge, Trusted Learning Advisors provide guidance and advice specific to the stakeholder's needs and objectives, while always striving to constantly create value.

Trusted Learning Advisors:

- Act as an agent on behalf of a stakeholder.
- Invest a lot of time and effort in getting to know the stakeholder.
- Become more aware of stakeholder needs and context.
- Consistently seek to add value to their stakeholders.
- Have the willingness and ability to challenge the stakeholder when necessary, to stand up and say, "There might be a better approach to solve this problem and here's why. Let me help you."

Trusted Learning Advisors are not in the business of telling stakeholders what to do. Trusted Learning Advisors are in the business of leading stakeholders to the right solution.

The Trusted Learning Advisor Value Proposition

What is the value that you can provide as a Trusted Learning Advisor? Simply put—you help your stakeholder get better results more efficiently, effectively, and systematically than they would have been able to achieve without you. **Your value proposition is utilizing your expertise to help stakeholders achieve their goals.** As a Trusted Learning Advisor, you create real, tangible, and measurable value—value that persists long after you finish the project.

The creation of value for the organization occurs through improved performance achieved by your ability to:

- leverage analysis to identify the root cause and solve the correct problems the first time, reducing time and money
- solve performance problems that result in increasing employee productivity and improve operational efficiency
- provide meaningful L&D opportunities which result in increasing employee growth, employee retention, and employee engagement

As Trusted Learning Advisors, your purpose is to drive impact which results in value creation for the organization.

The Need for Trusted Learning Advisors

If you are reading this book, I will already assume you at least have a feeling that there is a better way to do your job, to provide more value for your stakeholders, learners, and organization, and to feel like you have a purpose.

There is a better way—and you do have a greater purpose as an L&D practitioner.

L&D has a critically important role to play in the organization. The L&D function guides the capability of the organization, ultimately enabling it to grow. Organizations hire people to do specific jobs, but those jobs and the needs of the organization evolve over time. As the needs begin to evolve, the people also need to evolve, and that's where our creation of value exists.

L&D serves to support the shifts in evolution to ensure the organization can stay competitive. L&D exists to provide the frameworks, the tools, and the content to support the ability of the organization to continue to grow. Otherwise, the organization would continuously need to invest in new talent and capabilities, which can be extremely costly and time consuming. Through the L&D function, **you are developing talent to their fullest potential**. That is your purpose.

As an L&D practitioner, your role requires you to be a cross-functional business partner throughout the organization, which can mean you have many, many different stakeholders. It's a non-stop balancing act of managing stakeholder expectations while keeping L&D a priority in the business.

Our modern business paradigm demands that businesses be hyper-flexible and ready to respond to a myriad of unforeseen challenges. The key to this ability is a well-trained and adaptive workforce. Your learners and their potential, as well as the organization's welfare, depend on you breaking away from old paradigms.

When you are truly invested in your stakeholders' success, your stakeholders will be far more invested in **your** success.

It is only by demonstrating a measurable impact of your ability to be a consultative business partner with a keen focus on improving the company's performance and success that we can transform into Trusted Learning Advisors.

When stakeholders see you as a dynamic engine of growth and bring you into the decision-making inner circle—everyone wins.

Trusted Advisors Abound in Other Professions... Why Not L&D?

A Trusted Advisor is someone the business is comfortable with, intimate with, and has a trusted relationship with. A Trusted Advisor is someone respected for their knowledge and guidance, and provides advice, perspective, and information.

A Trusted Advisor is a skilled practitioner in their own business and the business of their stakeholders, is forward thinking, and sees what is happening while proactively working with the business to create solutions. Trusted Advisors help their stakeholders feel like they have a partner and a collaborator.

Think about your life and who you consider a Trusted Advisor. When you have a problem in a specific area, like taxes, your health, or your car, who do you call? And, more importantly, why do you call them? What makes that individual stand out from the others? Is it how they comfort you? Or is it a trust that they have your back and you know they are going to help you? Think about that feeling they give you. That feeling is what you want to give your stakeholders.

Trusted Advisors are plentiful in other professions, making the relative dearth of such a role in L&D all the more curious—and troubling.

Consider how attorneys, doctors, dentists, tax accountants, auto repair specialists, information technology professionals, and others perform in their roles and are perceived by their stakeholders. When the stakeholder approaches the Trusted Advisor, they may do so with their own prescribed solution, preferred outcome, or idea to be executed. Just think about how many times you have Googled your symptoms for a self-diagnosis. But when the Trusted Advisor gives guidance or direction... the stakeholder listens! After all, that's why they are there engaging them.

What Happens When People Don't Follow the Advice of Trusted Advisors in Other Professions?

The dental patient who does not follow a prescribed remedy from their dentist will likely be in pain until they can't stand it anymore, returning, and willing to take any action the dentist deems necessary to resolve the issue, aka pain. The auto repair customer might skip the recommended oil or spark plug change until their engine stops running and they come back pleading for a resolution. The doctor's patient who refuses to take the prescribed medications or guidance about changing harmful habits will soon find their ailments not improving... or worse.

The same applies with L&D professionals who are not treated as Trusted Advisors. When your stakeholders give orders for training programs and you willingly comply without a second thought, the solution often fails to provide the intended problem-solving outcome (maybe not always, but often enough). The stakeholder then returns enquiring why the learning program didn't fix the problem, calling it "your training solution"—knowing full well they prescribed the solution, and you simply executed it.

In many cases they ask for a new solution that doesn't vary much from the first—resulting in more time and money wasted on interventions with little return on investment. In the end, it's your reputation that is tarnished, regardless of who placed the order. Being an order taker not only puts your future at risk, it also threatens the future health of the organization.

Trusted Advisors have the backbone to say "no" to a stakeholder—in a diplomatic fashion—when they understand what the stakeholder wants is not in their best interest. Being a Trusted Learning Advisor requires suspending the instinct to immediately execute the order without due diligence. Oftentimes, your stakeholders are looking to L&D for a "quick fix" and instant gratification—neither of which are typical outcomes with learning initiatives.

Taking such a stance shows that L&D is willing to stand with its stakeholders as a thinking partner, collaborator, and peer—not simply as an order taker.

The Growing Risks of Not Evolving Into Trusted Learning Advisors

The greatest risk for L&D is to do nothing. If nothing changes… the status quo continues, and you continue to be perceived only as an order taker, which imposes an artificial ceiling on your ability to perform.

But the desire to evolve L&D into Trusted Learning Advisors is not merely one of our own self-interest. While there are benefits to us in terms of greater job satisfaction, purpose, and fulfillment, the overarching reason for such a metamorphosis should be to reduce the risk to organizations that comes from failing to accurately identify and address the root cause of problems that can drag down or even cripple organizational performance. Staying in the status quo undermines the overall potential for improved organizational performance.

Too often, acting as order takers results in your stakeholders having to fix the same problems repeatedly, and organizations finding themselves running in place while competitors with more evolved L&D organizations race past them in closing key performance gaps, creating innovative new products, improving employee retention, or reducing escalating costs. Perceiving and treating learning professionals as order takers leads to wasting money on learning interventions and programs that do little to address the root cause of many performance problems.

There are numerous reasons why L&D must evolve, many of which I will cover in Chapter 3. Until then, here is one case study to demonstrate the impact that can be achieved for both you and your stakeholders when you are able to perform as a Trusted Learning Advisor.

CASE STUDY

Why Trusted Learning Advisors Are Needed: A Real-World Case

Regardless of whether your company is a Fortune 500 company or a small startup, the challenge of being order takers is pervasive across organizations, industries, and geography. Take, for example, one large Fortune 500 global automobile manufacturer whose L&D organization recently went through a four-year transformational change from being order takers to Trusted Learning Advisors.

For years, learning operated as a decentralized function, driven by brand, business, or dealership needs. As a result, many duplicate efforts occurred, and significant opportunities existed to reduce cost and waste. The organization decided to form a learning Center of Excellence (COE) to centralize, streamline, and standardize the approach to learning with the intended outcome of providing cost savings and improved dealership performance.

Right from the start the center functioned as order takers (as many do when learning functions are just developing), adopting the mindset that because they were there to serve the business needs, they needed to do exactly what the business said. The team also didn't have the confidence or the experience to recognize the value-add they could provide as many had rotated into L&D as business subject matter experts (SMEs), not L&D practitioners.

The order-taking cycle went like this: the business would identify a problem; the business would conclude the problem could be solved through training; the business would contact their center of learning to submit a request; and the learning order would be executed as prescribed.

Rinse and repeat.

After operating in this manner for some time, the L&D group wanted to determine how its services were being perceived by its stakeholders. The group sought to run a survey and capture a net promoter score (NPS) from its partners to gauge the quality of service and partnership it was providing. Given that an NPS score of 50 is considered average, the results proved shocking to the L&D team—their stakeholders rated their service an NPS score of 33. The group had been operating under the assumption it was performing well since it had been doing exactly what the stakeholders wanted—simply executing the requested orders.

The survey results were the first inkling for L&D that their business partners did not see them as a strategic partner that could be relied on to help address and resolve pressing performance problems. Instead, the business believed the opposite, that L&D lacked innovation and consultative support.

The feedback proved to be a significant wake-up call for this L&D function. The learning leaders started putting a plan of action in place. The first data point identified that they wanted to resolve was to improve the L&D practitioner skills of the team, which would mean more knowledge and experience of necessary skills such as needs analysis, critical thinking, communication, measurement, and being innovative. Additionally, the team established tighter processes around order intake and project alignment.

Based on the stakeholders' feedback, the L&D team also recognized it needed to be more integrated into the business. An initiative was put together to have a concentrated focus on learning more about the business. Additionally, focus was placed to ensure stronger connections were being made between learning strategies and business strategies that would enable the team to demonstrate awareness and prioritization of business needs. The team also conducted research about competitors and industry trends, and shared that data in conversations with stakeholders to demonstrate a deeper awareness of the business with a forward-thinking mindset.

Slowly, the perception that the learning function were order takers began to change. For example, rather than having orders for learning programs dictated at the last minute, the business began to have discussions with learning and issue orders earlier in the communication process; this was progress. The next year the team conducted another stakeholder survey to capture the NPS and noticed the score started to rise slightly.

After the second year of being on the transformational journey to becoming Trusted Learning Advisors, the business began to ask L&D for its input on their proposed solutions to performance problems—a milestone that opened the door for L&D to become even more consultative. The team was now being invited to discussions proactively instead of reactively and communication was improving. As a result, cost savings were being recognized due to the reduction of redundant/repetitive learning development errors and timelines.

As the evolution continued during the third year, the L&D team formalized their approach to the idea of problem solving and innovation. They conducted qualitative research with learners and dealers and used the voice-of-the-customer data to drive their strategy. They also began conducting small prototypes of performance improvement initiatives that used design thinking methodology to help identify performance gaps and potential solutions. Once the prototypes seemed viable and there was data to back them up, L&D took the potential solutions back to the business to garner support to execute the solutions at a wider scale.

Rather than only trying to get a seat at the table with the business partners, the L&D team were setting their own table and inviting the business to join them. Both qualitative and quantitative data was now being produced to demonstrate L&D was having a positive impact on the business.

In year four of the transformation, stakeholders were now giving L&D far more time and space to conduct a thorough needs analysis before prescribing any solutions. And by the end of the year, the group's transformation from order takers to Trusted Learning Advisors was well on its way. The transformation was demonstrated and celebrated by several key factors:

- Improved return on investment (ROI) through an increase in vehicle sales due to product training programs.
- Reduction in the employee turnover rate due to an improved onboarding experience and new hire training programs.
- Accumulation of multiple industry awards.
- Streamlined processes reduced operational costs.

But the most important data point to demonstrate that the team's transformation was recognized by their stakeholders was indicated in how their business partners rated them in their latest survey. Four years prior, the team received an NPS of 33 which set them on the path of transformation. Now, their business partners rated them an NPS of 63, nearly doubling over the four-year period.

The L&D function was no longer perceived as or acting as order takers. Instead, they were deeply ingrained in the business, looking proactively for problems to solve even before the business was aware the problems existed and consistently driving value.

The L&D team learned to be able to quantify and qualify the value they produced for the business and articulate it in a way the business understood.

The transformation into Trusted Learning Advisors for this L&D function was achieved—although this status is never in a state of permanence; it's a continuous journey. L&D now had a seat at the table, was viewed as a consultative business partner, and was delivering measurable value to the business.

EXERCISE
Your Turn

Take a few moments and reflect on the previous case study. Are there any parallels between the case study and your experiences? Are there any examples you can pull from the case study to apply within your own organization?

Trusted Learning Advisors Are Not Overnight Sensations

As the example of the previous case study shows, the transition to becoming—and being perceived as—a Trusted Learning Advisor doesn't happen overnight. Stakeholders don't simply roll out the red carpet and anoint us as Trusted Learning Advisors on day one when we are setting our intentions to begin working differently.

A successful transition requires doing the hard work every day to overcome entrenched, historical views of L&D. It demands not only considerable resilience and persistence, but the courage of your convictions. It also means you will have to learn to walk the fine line between gently educating, influencing, and persuading impatient stakeholders of the need for process change without insulting their intelligence, but also knowing when to pick your battles—possibly even retreating so you can have the opportunity to continue the journey another day. More on this in Chapter 8.

Making the transformation into a Trusted Learning Advisor also means you'll need to learn to live in "two worlds" for a time. Your order-taking responsibilities won't simply disappear as your L&D department transitions to more of an advisory and consultative role.

It also can be true that your L&D group has not reached a maturity level where it's ready to begin transitioning to Trusted Learning Advisors. Your team may lack team members with the business acumen, learning science knowledge, consultative skills, or emotional intelligence needed to function successfully in the high-stakes role of Trusted Learning Advisor. Attempts to make that leap before the L&D function is fully prepared can set such ambitions back for years, since credibility and trust will be undermined if business partners perceive you are not yet equipped to assume such an influential role. I will cover this in depth in Chapter 7.

My hope is that these real, but surmountable, obstacles do not dissuade you or your L&D colleagues from seeking to become Trusted Learning Advisors. After all, this should be the aspirational goal of all L&D practitioners. However, many are not yet aware there is something more we should be... something more we can be. Becoming a Trusted Learning Advisor starts simply with the mindset of wanting to be more than what we are today.

Now you just need to keep reading and then apply what you've learned.

Remember

A Trusted Learning Advisor holds the key to unlocking performance-driven engagement and fostering creativity and innovation that erases the limits of what an organization can achieve. But to use the key, you need to show up for your organization—demonstrating your value as a consultative business partner by providing insight and actionable advice that links practical solutions to business strategy, effectively solving the problems, and consistently providing value.

In the next chapter I will review the current state of affairs for the L&D industry, examining how the practice of order taking took root and became the status quo in the L&D profession.

I will also explore the growing challenges facing organizations that require L&D's expertise and describe how those challenges can be better addressed by transforming into Trusted Learning Advisors.

KEY POINTS

- Today many are treated as order takers. Stakeholders identify a problem. Stakeholders identify a learning solution. Stakeholders give the order. And then we execute it. This stops today.

- Trusted Advisors exist in many fields (legal, medical, financial), and can (and will) exist in the field of L&D.

- A Trusted Learning Advisor is more than a learning provider—you are a strategic partner who can see your stakeholder's big picture and help them achieve it. You see how and why the solution fits, what the capabilities mean for long-term success, and how it can be implemented in the best possible way.

- When L&D evolves into Trusted Learning Advisors, we have stronger chances of executing on our vision for the talent and growth of the organization. Simply put, the L&D function serves the development of an organization's most important asset—the employees.

- The value proposition of Trusted Learning Advisors is utilizing your expertise to help stakeholders achieve their goals. As a Trusted Learning Advisor, you create real, tangible, and measurable value— value that persists long after you finish the project.

- Without L&D acting in the role of Trusted Learning Advisors, organizations will continue to waste money on learning interventions that do little to address the real underlying causes of performance and organizational challenges, too often requiring that leaders have to fix the same problems over and over again.

- Trusted Learning Advisors drive impact which results in creating value for the organization.

Understanding Order Takers: The Current State of Affairs

02

"If you don't know where you come from, it's difficult to determine where you are. It's even more difficult to plan where you are going."

JOSEPH LOWERY

How We Got Here: A Brief History of Order Taking

Today the Learning & Development (L&D) industry is recognized as and treated like order takers. You know this already; you face it every day. But what you may not know is that order taking is not a recent phenomenon in the field of L&D. In the United States, the practice of order taking in the organizational training environment can be traced as far back as the Industrial Revolution (18th/19th century).

Stick with me—the history is important. If you don't know where you are today or how you got here, you won't know how to get to where you want to go tomorrow. So, before we dive deeper into the future state of being Trusted Learning Advisors, let's take a step back and explore how we got here.

The management theorists and corporate titans of the Industrial Revolution era believed workers were largely subservient and needed to be controlled through enforced methods. In other words, factory workers needed to be told (trained) on exactly what to do. That philosophy was woven through the mass production techniques introduced by Henry Ford of the Ford Motor Company, which revolutionized business practices of the time.

From that power dynamic emanated the belief that those responsible for training workers on the front lines should take orders from business managers on what needed to be taught (is this sounding familiar?). The thinking among Ford and Frederick Winslow Taylor, the influential author of a seminal book in that period called *The Principles of Scientific Management* (1911), was that only managers were capable of specifying how work tasks should be accomplished and how performance problems should be solved, imbuing the *control and command-* type power that business continues to hold today.

Overcoming Stereotypes

When you consider it was more than a century ago that the practice of treating learning practitioners as order takers took root in the United States, and that it has continued unabated to this day, it's easier to understand the considerable challenge the L&D profession faces on our evolutionary journey to becoming Trusted Learning Advisors.

Changing stereotypes first requires understanding the conditions and theories that created such belief systems, then doing the hard daily work of reshaping perceptions and creating new narratives.

In the 18th and 19th centuries, training within organizations, or corporate schools, was intended to be used to maintain control and power over workers, specifically factory workers in the textile, steel, coal, and automotive industries.[1] The intention was to create docile and obedient workers who did exactly what they were told. Management specified the way in which work tasks would be accomplished and created training to ensure workers followed in stride. Formal training functions emerged to support the necessary training.

In 1872, printing press company Hoe and Co. created the first classroom-based organizational training when it built a school to train machinists. A few decades later the National Cash Register

Company introduced the first HR department—then known as a personnel function—in response to worker strikes and lockouts. That department was focused on record keeping, handling employee grievances and wage management, and it later constructed a schoolhouse for employee education. Fun fact—the schoolhouse was where the first documented sales training programs were delivered.

Ford put his own spin on the emerging concept of HR by creating a "sociological department" at the Ford Motor Company in 1913. As part of this new department, Ford ordered the creation of training programs that would help his workers build automobiles better, faster and cheaper. He encouraged his trainers to apply principles from Taylor's recently published book, which described new ways to optimize, standardize, and simplify jobs to maximize productivity.

It's within Taylor's theories where one gets a glimpse into the beginnings of order taking in L&D. As more "corporate schools" arose in the early 1900s, they became enamored with Taylor's scientific management approach. According to Altman (2008), an academic researcher who traced the history of "employer-dominated education and training," in using Taylor's approach managers and engineers would precisely specify the way work tasks should be accomplished by employees.[2]

"Worker input was not important, and workers needed only be trained in these specific tasks," Altman wrote in his study. Given that managers and supervisors were the ones who controlled and managed the way work was done, workplace training favored their roles over the role of the worker. Most notably, the corporate schools of that era gave management—not training practitioners—complete control in how workers would be trained.

Order Taking as "Settled Law"

It was amid the widespread adoption of Taylor's and Ford's theories during the Industrial Revolution that order taking became the equivalent of "settled law."

The business was positioned by leaders of the era as all-knowing, innovative, and the lifeblood of company success. Training departments, on the other hand, were seen as subordinate to the line's needs, expected to be deferential and leap into action when summoned to build whatever training business leaders ordered to keep the assembly lines humming and profit levels high. (Ringing any bells?)

As the decades passed following the Industrial Revolution, academics began to conduct more theory-based research into L&D, theories which started to replace some of the trial-and-error learning practices occurring in manufacturing plants, warehouses, and offices.

During World War II, the TWI (Training Within Industry) Service, a nationwide partnership between industry and the U.S. War Manpower Commission, had helped rapidly scale up production of military equipment and trained millions of new workers. TWI helped establish technical training programs in thousands of manufacturing plants after WWII, using new strategies such as the four-step job instruction program.[3]

The period just after World War II in the late 1940s, for example, saw growing demand for trained workers because of an expanding economy and innovations in technology. Individualized instruction became prominent in these years, a practice which replaced instructors with material that broke learning into small steps with follow-up activities to check comprehension.

Progress continued in the 1950s when Professor Donald Kirkpatrick published his landmark Four Levels of Learning Evaluation, which took the measurement of learning impact beyond "did they like it?" to "did it impact the bottom line?"

The 1970s saw Malcolm Knowles introduce his theory of andragogy, which posits that adults learn in very different ways than children.

The 1980s were highlighted by the creation of ADDIE (Analysis, Design, Development, Implementation and Evaluation), which became the foundation for modern instructional design. About the same time the CEO of Motorola Corp. decided that for his company to survive in an increasingly competitive global marketplace each employee needed new skills. He built the landmark Motorola University, partnering with area community colleges and focusing on teaching employees basic literacy and math.

Although this move was a risky investment, it paid off, giving Motorola a competitive edge and serving as an indicator that effective L&D had a significant general education component.

It can be said that prior to World War II, training within organizations focused on command and control of workers through vocational skills, whereas after the war workforce training started to shift to focus on the workers, including skills that would benefit them personally. Management started to view workers as people instead of another cog in the production process, which began to formalize the field of human resource development (HRD).[4]

It wasn't until the early 1980s that Taylorism started to lose support within organizations as profits and productivity were in decline as a result of global competition and technological change.[5] Organizations recognized workers needed additional skills beyond those supported under Taylorism, such as analytical, verbal, and quantitative skills.

There are more practitioners and academics that influenced the evolution in the period between 1960—2000, but to identify them all would turn this chapter into an encyclopedia. My intention was to briefly cover some of the key influencers/activities that occurred—not to put you to sleep with a cavernous history lesson.

One Constant Amid Change: Order Taking

Through the 1980s and beyond, order taking rolled on largely unchallenged as an accepted operating paradigm even as the L&D field abandoned other ineffective or outdated strategies in favor of improved approaches.

In the 1990s organizations began to introduce computer-based training and the concept of blended learning—creating a mix of online and in-person instruction to optimize benefits of each method—gained popularity

The period from 2000 through to today was characterized by the rise of technologies like learning management systems (LMSs), the morphing of eLearning into "micro-learning" instructional design approaches, and more recently the widespread adoption of mobile learning, which enables employees to access learning from anywhere at any time, transforming how training is designed and delivered. Virtual reality (VR), augmented reality (AR), Learner Experience Platforms (LXP), and chatbots, to name a few, are other technology learning enablers on the rise.

Despite myriad improvements since the Industrial Revolution, L&D has continued to function in a largely reactive role, allowing the business to define performance problems and choose solutions with little front-end consultation from those with the most expertise and training in those areas—seasoned L&D practitioners. As technology has advanced and allowed L&D to create more accessible and impactful learning experiences within the flow of work, one singular practice remains stubbornly stuck in the past—order taking.

Even with time, order taking hasn't gone away, it's simply taken on new forms over the decades. Today business leaders knock on L&D's door, not so much to order classroom training but rather to demand a 30-minute web-based course, a short instructional video, or perhaps "gamified" learning content to help address problems such as lagging sales, communication problems on their teams, or because last quarter's customer satisfaction numbers took a troublesome dip.

The idea that took root more than a century ago that L&D's role is subservient to the business—not one of equal partners in identifying and closing key skill or performance gaps—continues to persist today even in light of the many advances and innovations made by L&D practices.

But, again, you probably already know this.

Organizational Factors Contributing to the Role of Order Takers

That was the past. Fast-forward to today... two key organizational factors continue to play a role contributing to the perception L&D

are order takers: organizational culture and organizational placement. This is important for you to understand as you should be striving to influence the organizational culture and be aware of how the organizational placement of L&D can impact your work.

Organizational Culture

Organizational culture is defined as a system of assumptions, values, norms, and attitudes developed within an organization which help employees determine how to behave in that organization.[6] Essentially, culture defines what is important to an organization and, as a result, impacts every action, decision, or interaction in the organization.

Research has shown the mechanism of organizational culture is one of the most central and important elements in determining whether learning is encouraged or discouraged throughout an organization.[7] Assumptions, norms, values, and attitudes, all attributes of organizational culture, impact, stimulate, and shape the behaviors toward organizational learning.

Starting at the top and working its way down through the organization, the culture can contribute towards the limitations of L&D being restricted to those of order takers. If the organization does not have a learning culture, does not place value on L&D, or if the C-suite (high-ranking executives) do not support learning, L&D can be very limited in their ability to execute anything beyond the orders received.

Although potentially a challenging task, it's important to recognize the maturity level of executive leadership, stakeholders, and the culture as it relates to learning. I've worked in several organizations where leadership did not support or promote learning. Regardless of how much effort we put into creating a learning culture, if leadership did not make it part of the business strategy or business priorities, we have very little ability to influence frontline management to provide learning opportunities for their teams and ultimately to change the perception of our stakeholders from one of viewing us as strictly order takers.

Does your organization support a learning culture?

Organizational Placement

Where the L&D organization sits within the organizational hierarchy can influence the perception of L&D being order takers. For example, whether L&D sits inside the human resources function rather than as a separate business unit—or whether each business unit has its own L&D structure—can affect how the L&D function is perceived and the type of restraints Trusted Learning Advisors are forced to operate under.

When L&D sits within or under another function, L&D can be treated like order takers within those functions, sometimes out of fear. If L&D is too creative or gets too close to the stakeholder, other people, such as account managers, might feel threatened that their own value and role are at risk.

Sanjo, a 15-year L&D practitioner, described to me the navigational challenge of the L&D organizational structure he has faced as the following:

> Exploring potential barriers to our success for being Trusted Learning Advisors can start by looking in our backyard and asking, "How does HR view L&D?" When L&D sits within HR, sometimes HR blocks those relationships. If you want to talk to a business leader, you must go through HR. In some instances, this type of hierarchy can make it harder for L&D to be a Trusted Learning Advisor.
>
> In some organizations I had free range and free access to the business leaders. As they came to our programs, I interacted with them. I could follow up with them and ask them questions. When I was out traveling, I could meet with them and spend time with them.
>
> In my next organization, when L&D sat within HR, it was much more restrictive. Every discussion and engagement with a business leader had to go through HR, putting a layer of complexity on L&D being recognized as a strategic partner.

Another organizational construct that can influence the perception of L&D is whether L&D is structured as a support function (cost center) or as a line of business that makes money (profit center). Having L&D structured as a support function often influences the belief that L&D has a lower value association since it "costs" the business money and can result in business treating L&D as order takers. When

L&D is a cost center, it can feel like we are constantly trying to justify our position, value, and our existence within the organization as a result.

Thank you for giving me time to cover the historical background on order taking. It's important to understand how we got here. The more academic portion of the chapter is complete, and now we can focus on how we are being impacted today.

EXERCISE
Your Turn

Think about the organizational culture and organizational construct in your current organization. Can you identify whether the culture or construct is supporting or inhibiting the role of L&D? Can you identify any other factors that may be contributing to your organization viewing L&D as order takers?

Understanding Order Takers

Although I'm quite confident you understand what an order taker is, just to make sure we have the same understanding, I'll give a brief explanation. In L&D, being an order taker is reflective when the stakeholder asks us to accomplish a task, usually with certain restraints. The order can feel like a prescription for an unknown, unidentified, or unexplored problem. As an order taker, we execute the order as-is even when we sometimes already know it will not impact the underlined problem.

Although the foundations of organizational L&D are rooted in stakeholders giving orders (as you learned in the previous pages), we are also one of the reasons the default view of L&D continues to be order taking—particularly because we subscribe to the same default view of ourselves, at least early in our career. For most of us in L&D, we started as order takers for one simple reason: we did not know better.

Loren Sanders, CVS learning leader and Trusted Learning Advisor, shared with me her perspective on why she started as an order taker:

> "When I started in L&D, I took orders because I didn't know any different. I didn't know at the time what questions I should be asking. I was doing as I was told, because I was told to. It didn't even occur to me at the time that I should ask questions, that I should gather more information."

Like Loren, I started as an order taker for no other reason than I simply didn't know any different. No one told me I had permission to think critically, explore alternative solutions, or act as a consultative business partner. My younger self blames my older self for not having this book available to guide me to a different path.

During my first five years in the industry, all the teams I was part of were order takers. How would I have known to behave any differently? Who would have taught me? This might sound familiar to you too—either with your past or current experience. Possibly no one has told you that you have permission to be a valuable contributing business partner to your stakeholders. Maybe no one told you that your experience, point of view, and voice matter. (They do, by the way.) But now you are learning there is a different way, a better way for you, your stakeholders, and your learners. And if no one has yet given you permission to start acting like a Trusted Learning Advisor, please accept this book as your permission.

But even after all of this, even once we do become aware there is another way, a better way—some remain as order takers.

Why?

Acting as an order taker seems easier than being a Trusted Learning Advisor, and in a way, it is—at least at first. Like we saw with Julia, she grew exhausted with the resistance and pushback from stakeholders. As an order taker, there is definitely less resistance. And an order taker doesn't really have to think—someone else has determined the solution, they've communicated it to you, and now you simply need to execute it. It feels like there is less accountability, less ownership.

On the flip side, being a Trusted Learning Advisor requires us to assume the full burden of responsibility for the effectiveness of our programs, to navigate skillfully the headwinds of resistance, to educate the stakeholders and to bring about a meaningful change.

Taking the order and limiting our roles to executors appears more expedient. It's easier to take the order and default to "I would love to design an amazing workshop or training session for you" in response. In contrast, as a Trusted Learning Advisor, you must first go through the hard work of figuring out if a proposed L&D program is rationally connected to the issue it is intended to fix. If such a connection does not exist, if the "L&D fix" serves no logical purpose, then you have an ethical, quasi-fiduciary duty to our profession and our stakeholders to say that.

Being a Trusted Learning Advisor requires commitment and effort. You might sometimes feel overwhelmed by the notion of "lack of time" to embrace this role, given its demanding nature. However, I would argue that you cannot afford to sideline your duties as a Trusted Learning Advisor. Consider the significant future effort required to rectify complications if a program fails, behaviors remain unaltered, or operational issues persist unresolved. Add to this the consequent waste of time and money, not to mention the reputational and relational damage that could ensue. No matter the workload you face when an order comes in, it becomes crucial to carve out the necessary time to do your due diligence as a Trusted Learning Advisor and execute successfully the first time. This will be discussed in more detail in Chapter 8. But first, it's important to understand the order.

EXERCISE
Your Turn

Now that you understand more about order taking, take a few moments to identify factors that contributed to you initially adopting an order taker mindset. Are there any factors remaining that you need to overcome?

Understanding the Order

It took me a long time to realize that behind the order being given by the stakeholder was a message. And it was my responsibility to try to decode the message. Understanding the order starts with understanding the stakeholder.

It's important to keep in mind that your stakeholder may also be an order taker (order taking isn't beholden only to L&D). Very likely someone has told your stakeholder a problem and prescribed the solution, and they are passing it along. I've had countless orders where, after further investigation, I uncovered someone else told someone else who eventually told my stakeholder who then relayed it to me—like the old game of telephone. "My boss's boss told me to do this, can you just get it done?" Which can be one of the reasons why by the time it reaches you, something may have been lost in translation along the way, further emphasizing the importance for you to conduct your due diligence. Your stakeholders can also be in uncomfortable situations which is why it's important to understand the "why" behind the order and how it originated. (More on intake and needs analysis later!)

Symptoms

The orders you receive can sometimes sound like fully baked ideas with executable tasks aimed to solve organizational issues. And it's possible that's true on occasion. But more often than not, your stakeholders are providing you with the symptoms of the problem. The symptom of the problem is employee retention, low employee engagement, lack of data in the system, declining profits, increased operation costs, or an influx of accidents or safety issues. Those are all symptoms of a problem.

Imagine this... you just stepped off the street curb and lost your balance. Quickly catching yourself from falling, you put your foot on the ground but in an awkward position, something just not right. Immediately you feel a rush of pain shoot up through your foot and it doesn't stop. Trying to keep the pressure off your foot, you hobble back home and take two Tylenol for the pain. You grab a bag of frozen vegetables from the freezer, an extra pillow and lay yourself on the sofa while elevating and veggie-icing your foot.

The next day you are elevating your foot and taking Tylenol, but you are also continuing your normal routine of walking to work (albeit painfully). You come home, take your pills, elevate your foot, and continue this routine.

After four weeks you realize the pain is not improving. Reluctantly you go to the doctor (after all, they are your Trusted Advisor) and get an x-ray to uncover you have a hairline fracture—but not where you thought it was (or thought you felt it). The closest nerve endings for the break were in your foot—turns out the fracture is in your ankle. By continuing to walk on it, the break was exacerbated and now you might need to have your ankle reset and start the healing process over from the beginning.

Each day you were masking the problem you thought you had (the foot) by only addressing the symptoms with Tylenol and elevation, but by continuing your normal routine, you were keeping the real problem (your ankle) from healing properly. This is the lifecycle of order taking in L&D. (This is also a semi-autobiographical description of why it took me months to uncover that I had a broken leg and that my doctor was NOT a Trusted Advisor—but that's another story.)

Each time you take an order without the proper diagnosis, you continue this metaphorical cycle. Not only is it easy to have the pain of the problem felt elsewhere, deflecting from the actual root cause, but each time you take the proverbial Tylenol and continue walking on your foot (execute on the order), you risk exacerbating the real problem. As a result, you are potentially wasting time, money, resources, risking your reputation, and further limiting the impact L&D can have on the organization and the value you can provide to your stakeholders and your learners.

In Action

Earlier in my career I remember talking with the Chief Financial Officer (CFO) of a small company regarding a problem she was facing. As she explained it, she was responsible for understanding the financial value and revenue throughout the company and needed to have a clear pipeline of potential sales.

Her challenge was her inability to accurately project or summarize the current state of the business. More specifically, she did not have insight into the sales pipeline, and it was having a trickle-down effect on reporting challenges in other parts of the business. Without it, she explained, forecasting all the way down to managing the pipeline of talent necessary to support the business could not be successfully completed, impacting the bottom line. The reason for the challenge, according to her, was that the sales team was not using the customer relationship management (CRM) system. Therefore, the solution, according to her, must be to provide training on the CRM system for the sales team.

As an order taker, it sounds logical—after all, I didn't know anything about finance and how the processes work for their company. I had two choices—execute the order, or spend a little time with the sales team to understand them and their working processes first. I chose the second option.

After interviewing nine members of the sales team, I learned that they were all very well versed in using the CRM system. They knew exactly how the functions and features worked and where the data went; they even gave me a crash course to see it in action. What I uncovered, however, was that the team simply was not motivated to fill out the CRM. "It takes 30 minutes out of my day that I could be out selling. It's a pain to fill out. And besides, I get my commission regardless."

Not inputting data into the CRM is a behavioral, operational, and process issue. Systems training was not the answer—they already knew the system. Rather, what was needed was to help the sales consultants see the bigger picture—their failure to input data had a direct impact on others. If the order data is not put into the system, it has a downstream impact on other parts of the organization. For example, Recruitment does not have line of sight for how many resources they need to source, Finance can't forecast, and Operations can't plan properly.

Although training could help the sales consultants see the larger picture, training was not the solution. In this case, the solution was process and communication. One solution could be putting a process in place to hold sales consultants accountable for entering data and giving them key performance indicators (KPIs) to be measured against. Another option was changing the pay model to incentivize

Sales to enter target data, linking it back to their KPIs. A third option was having their leadership communicate to them their expectations, and why it was important.

Regardless of the approach, the issue this organization faced was not a training issue. The problem, as the CFO understood it, was only a symptom of a larger issue. Luckily, I didn't just execute on the order and put the sales team through training on a system they already knew—wasting everyone's time and money. My approach and analysis helped the CFO see me as a Trusted Learning Advisor.

To fully understand the problem or situation, you need to look past the order addressing the symptom which masks the problem, and dig into the underlined root cause instead. This is often easier said than done. But don't worry, I will provide strategies and tactics on this in more detail in upcoming chapters.

Constraints

Not every order comes across clearly as an order. Sometimes your stakeholders will give you something that looks like an opportunity for you to be their Trusted Learning Advisor, sharing with you the organizational challenge, giving you an opportunity to conduct due diligence research and talk with learners, and even giving you a flexible timeline to complete the work. You start getting excited that your skillsets are finally being utilized... until they start putting on guardrails and requirements—otherwise known as constraints.

A constraint is something that limits or controls what you can do and can turn a consultative opportunity into a thinly veiled order.

The following are common examples of constraints given by stakeholders which limit your ability to provide expert support:

- Determining program characteristics ("I have specific content I want you to use" or "I want this to only be web-based training on the LMS").
- Determining the length of the program ("I want a one-day instructor-led training" or "We need a 20-minute web-based training").

- Determining the budget ("Keep the cost under $3,000 for the program" or "I don't want to spend more than $50 per person").
- Determining the development and deployment timelines ("This needs to be developed in the next two weeks" or "Everyone needs to be trained before Q3").

Although our stakeholders may have timeline and budget requirements which need to be considered, they still qualify as constraints.

One story Jorge, a fellow L&D practitioner, shared with me comes to mind when I think about constraints being used to limit the consulting ability of his team:

Not too long ago the business engaged my team to create a program for a new topic on customer experience. They made a strong business case for why customer experience was a problem, and even went as far as providing a book they wanted the team to use as the source material for the content development of the program. At first, providing material to use as content for the program might seem helpful, but it turned out to be one of several constraints on their order. The book they provided was a good book, but it was only one approach for customer experience. It created a bit of bias in the design by limiting our perspective to only the ideas and approaches in the book.

The next constraint they provided was the requirement that the program could only be delivered as an eLearning program. This would not have been our recommended approach. We would have recommended a hybrid approach with live and digital components to strengthen understanding of the material as well as roleplaying opportunities.

In trying to stick with an eLearning program and incorporate all the topics they prescribed, the course ended up being 120 minutes in length. This is longer than we would recommend for an eLearning course, and was the longest program we had ever created. The average eLearning course in our environment was 14 minutes.

The last constraint was that the business wanted everyone to complete the program within 30 days, even though the rollout would fall in December, which means many employees are taking time off for the holidays.

Our team set off to do our job even with the content, delivery modality, and deployment timeline constraints. We ended up meeting all the project requirements (constraints) set out by the business and rolled out the program on time and on budget with the content provided and through the modality requested. The feedback from the learners was positive and by meeting all their constraints, the business considered this a successful program. Until, however, the CEO reached out to my team to suggest we should have broken the content into smaller chunks and rolled the program out over the course of several months rather than trying to "cram it in at once."

I was speechless. We had done exactly what the business asked. The CEO was even part of the steering committee for the program, meaning he knew in real-time about the project constraints as they were being delivered to us. We had no real control over the project, and now we were being told the requirements we followed were wrong and it was somehow our responsibility.

In hindsight, the feedback from the CEO wasn't wrong. We knew having it be a long eLearning program, using only the book as the content, and forcing quick completion at the end of the year was not the right approach. It didn't feel right. But we didn't speak up; that's on us. We inadvertently continued the behavior that we were order takers. Although I'm not sure if we would have been able to influence the business one way or another, the reality is we didn't try. But that's also because of how the order came in—through my manager. The message was basically "We've got a new initiative and the CEO says it's important and it needs to launch." There's always this fear that comes with messages like that. But again, it's on us. We must change that mindset and it's not easy.

It's a slow work-in-progress evolution.

When we act like order takers, we are acting like bystanders, sitting on the sidelines waiting for someone to tell us what to do. Acting only as an order taker is enormously debilitating to our practice. Order taking disrespects and marginalizes the power of learning and the power of transformation it can have in organizations. It negates your value as a practitioner. I don't know about you, but when I'm acting like or treated like an order taker, I can feel it.

One of the best barometers we can use to help us decipher if we are being order takers is the voice inside our heads or the feeling inside our chest. As Britney Cole, one of my L&D confidants and Trusted Learning Advisor, once said to me, "If it's a drain to build it, it's a drain for the learner to complete it. If it feels wrong, it probably is."

Listen for the Voice. Trust Yourself.

Regardless of the many reasons why we became order takers, the fact of the matter is that many of us are still stuck in the order taking mindset. That's okay. Awareness is the first step to change.

We know being an order taker devalues our craft. It doesn't feel good.

You know this. I know this.

So why do we enable this behavior?

We lack the fundamental consultative skillsets necessary to say "no" without saying no, to demonstrate our credibility, establish trust, build the necessary relationships, and illustrate our value—all of which are topics covered in the remaining chapters.

Hopefully after this chapter, you now have a better understanding of how we got to where we are today. It wasn't you. It wasn't me. It started at the very beginning of our industry being created and it has persisted throughout... until now. And if you didn't already, you should also now have a thorough understanding of what being an order taker means and reasons why our organizations are still setting us up to be order takers.

Awareness, understanding, and knowledge empower you to drive change.

You have the greatest opportunity ahead of you—to evolve into Trusted Learning Advisors. The choice is yours. By reading this book and developing your skills, you are headed down the path for this transformational journey.

I hope by now you are recognizing there is a need for change, but I also don't want to assume you are feeling that passion, fire, or drive that is needed to fuel the journey. That's why I've dedicated the next chapter to really articulating and reinforcing why you need to make the commitment and put in the work necessary to evolve into Trusted Learning Advisors.

KEY POINTS

- L&D's history of functioning as order takers can be traced back to the creation of the first formal training functions established during the Industrial Revolution in the United States.

- Corporate schools of the 1900s gave management—not training practitioners—complete control over how workers would be trained, establishing the order taker practice.

- Despite numerous advances in learning theory, learning delivery practices, and the introduction of innovative new learning technologies, one L&D practice remains stubbornly stuck in the past: order taking.

- Trusted Learning Advisors are far better equipped to help companies tackle the daunting challenges they face today and will in the future.

- There is a message behind the order—find out what it is.

- Listen to the voice in your head, trust the feeling inside. If it feels wrong, it probably is wrong. That's the Trusted Learning Advisor inside you clamoring to get out into the world.

Endnotes

1 B A Altman. *The History of Workplace Learning in the United States and the Question of Control: A Selective Review of the Literature and the Implications of a Constructivist Paradigm*, 2008. Online submission.

2 B A Altman. *The History of Workplace Learning in the United States and the Question of Control: A Selective Review of the Literature and the Implications of a Constructivist Paradigm*, 2008. Online submission.

3 R J Torraco. Early history of the fields of practice of training and development and organization development, *Advances in Developing Human Resources*, 2016,18(4), 439–53

4 C F Anderson. *An historical approach to the relationship between adult education and the workplace: Path to empowerment in the 80s*, 1980. Doctoral dissertation, University of Michigan, Ann Arbor, MI

5 H Harris (2000) *Defining the future or reliving the past? Unions, employers, and the challenge of workplace learning*, ERIC Clearinghouse on Adult, Career, and Vocational Education, Columbus, OH

6 J L Campbell and A S Göritz. Culture corrupts! A qualitative study of organizational culture in corrupt organizations, *Journal of Business Ethics*, 2014, 120(3), 291–311

7 Econstor. Impact of Organizational Culture on Organizational Learning and Knowledge Management, 2015, www.econstor.eu/bitstream/10419/183644/1/22-ENT-2015-Janicijevic-pp-159-165.pdf (archived at https://perma.cc/H557-8GXD)

The Need to Evolve

03

"It is not the most intellectual of the species that survives; it is not the strongest that survives; but the species that survives is the one that is able best to adapt and adjust to the changing environment in which it finds itself."

CHARLES DARWIN

Depending on where you are in your career (just starting out vs seasoned) or your level of passion for the field of Learning & Development (it's a job vs meaningful work), you might not yet feel the fire necessary to incite change.

That's okay.

My job (and my passion) is to help you see the need to change.

Or maybe you **do** want to change, but you want more data and understanding to strengthen your arguments. I get that too!

Let me share with you why it is necessary to start your evolution into a Trusted Learning Advisor and to do it now. It starts with one word—change.

Change is constant. Change is all around us. Some even argue the speed at which change is happening is faster than ever. Volatility, uncertainty, complexity, and ambiguity (VUCA) have become the status quo in the evolving nature in which businesses operate and the way humans live their lives. A shift in demographics within the labor market, rapid urbanization in developing countries, economic power shifts, and the push for globalization are changing the fundamental way that businesses operate. Technology has revolutionized the workplace and the way we work.

People change. Technology changes. Industries change. Therefore, organizations need to change. And change within the organizational framework is executed by the people within the organization, which is where we, L&D come in, as the underpinning support mechanism to help our talent be agile, adapt, and evolve.

Although we know the L&D function is an enabler of talent success, if we do not evolve alongside or ahead of our business and talent, we may not have the opportunity to demonstrate the full breadth of our capabilities because we won't be around to do so.

Today there are three major drivers supporting the need for L&D to evolve into Trusted Learning Advisors:

1 Our self-preservation

2 The looming skills gap

3 The talent engagement and retention crisis

Our Self-Preservation

During my research on the topic of the evolution of L&D, I spoke with one of my mentors, author, professor, and Trusted Learning Advisor, Dr. Nigel Paine. Dr. Paine shared the following insight:

> The need for L&D to step up, to be empowered, to stop taking orders and begin to act as Trusted Learning Advisors has been a challenge for the last many years but nothing much has changed. The reality is—it takes two to tango. It's not just the business's fault for treating L&D like order takers. There are plenty of people in L&D who are happy and comfortable in that order-taking role and believing there is virtue in it. I find it quite depressing that nothing much has changed. To preserve our role and value in the organization, L&D must evolve into Trusted Learning Advisors.

> Self-preservation is the set of behaviors exhibited to ensure the survival of an organism. Our need to evolve into Trusted Learning Advisors starts as self-preservation for our role within the workplace.

The order taking mentality of L&D has been a challenge for the last many years. You now know, based on Chapter 2, that the L&D

function have always been order takers since the inception of our organizational function. If we want to survive as an industry, as a function within organizations, evolution is necessary.

If you are not producing value, as with any function in an organization, you become at risk.

Why?

Your stakeholders and businesses have a decision for their L&D needs. They have options. They can choose to use you or not. Finance can choose to continue investing in the internal L&D function or siphon those funds elsewhere if you are not demonstrating value. To provide value, you need to be using your L&D tools and your craft to serve your stakeholders and your learners—conducting needs analyses, applying the science of learning, connecting outcomes with business goals—all of which is your job as an L&D practitioner—and your role as a Trusted Learning Advisor.

As an order taker, you relinquish the opportunity to provide strategic influence because you are just doing what the business says by fulfilling their order. You undermine your own power, or whatever power you could have had, when you sit quietly and take the orders without providing any consultative behaviors.

Accepting the role of order taker means you do not carry yourself as a broader support function with the confidence or the gravitas to support the business equally.

Your evolution is necessary for your survival.

Technology evolves. Businesses evolve. People evolve. L&D needs to evolve.

Burnout

Self-preservation does not only mean preserving our industry; it also means preserving ourselves as individual L&D practitioners. One of the most pressing reasons we need to evolve is personal and self-serving.

As an L&D practitioner who is passionate about using the craft to better the lives of learners, feeling that you are "just" an order taker is discouraging and limiting. I liken it to a feeling of anxiety—restrained, with a weight on my chest making it difficult to breathe.

I know I have more to offer, and I know I can add value, but others are not willing to listen. I have a point of view, I have experience, I am a practitioner, but those skills are not being utilized.

Does this feel familiar?

Talking to my colleagues and fellow practitioners, I know I'm not alone in the restricted feeling resulting from being treated like an order taker. It does not feel good.

One of the greatest risks for L&D when we are treated like and act like order takers is burnout. Burnout is a type of work-related stress, typically resulting in a state of emotional, physical, and mental exhaustion. When a worker is feeling "burned out," they can experience an energy depletion resulting in extinction of motivation or incentive to do any work. Burnout doesn't just impact the workplace, but can spill out into other aspects of the worker's life.

Remember Julia from Chapter 1—when she lost the energy she started with because she was constantly met with resistance and unable to feel like she was fulfilling her purpose and use her skills, she was a victim of burnout. I've been there... many times. And I imagine you have too.

If we are constantly told what to do, how to do it, feel under-appreciated, and feel a lack of control, we start to shut down and lose our creativity, passion, and motivation. We start to limit the application of our practitioner skills, question the value of our role, and shut down. It can go as far as impacting our self-worth, which can ultimately lead to disengagement and attrition.

Disengagement leads to a poor-quality product being received by the business, which impacts L&D's reputation. It becomes a vicious cycle. The business isn't receiving the outcomes they expected from L&D and now they are putting on more pressure, dictating more orders to close our own performance gaps, all the while becoming more and more frustrated with us. As a result, we are not operating in an ideal state and we can't provide the business with the solutions they think they need, much less the solutions they actually need. They see zero value-add from us and when it's time to cut costs, we are first up on the chopping block.

Being treated as a Trusted Learning Advisor feels empowering and refreshing when we can do our job. It's as simple as that—we just want to be able to do our job, but unfortunately we have years of preconceived notions and inhibiting behaviors that we need to break through for our stakeholders to recognize our capabilities, our potential, and our impact.

One of the many things we learned about organizations through the global Covid-19 pandemic in 2020 is that the world can change overnight, resulting in the need for organizations and workers to adapt—also overnight. The pandemic forced L&D, as it did most other business units, to quickly evolve to address market needs.

By some measures, L&D is more highly valued than it's ever been. LinkedIn's 2022 Workplace Learning report found that 72 percent of respondents believe L&D is perceived as a more strategic function in their organizations today, in part owing to L&D' having met high expectations during Covid-19 in helping employees pivot to pandemic protocols, remote work, and hybrid operating models.[1]

Organizations have taken notice of the support we provided and the value we brought during their time of crisis. Now we need to continue our evolution while we have their attention and support.

Reputational Damage

Part of our self-preservation is protecting our reputation. By not evolving to Trusted Learning Advisors, our reputation suffers.

When L&D behaves like an order taker, it infantilizes our profession and hinders us from achieving our full potential. Enabling the order taker behavior furthers the formation of people who have no real understanding of L&D because they're just doing what they're told. We risk demeaning ourselves by remaining order takers, becoming nothing more than an input producing an output—like robots.

Part of the mission of L&D is to be critical thinkers and problem solvers. If we remove that from the equation and if we are not performing creative problem solving or critical thinking, it's fair to ask why our function within the organization continues to exist.

When we can't fully use our expertise, the reputation of the L&D profession suffers, and we grow even more vulnerable to the budgetary ax. When we're viewed as transactional order takers, we're considered more expendable or easily replaceable. But when we're seen as Trusted Learning Advisors whose expertise and advice are invaluable in helping to quickly diagnose problems and produce solutions in ways that reduce costs, boost productivity, or enhance revenue, we move into the ranks of pivotal strategic partners with elevated standing in the organization.

Research has shown L&D's efforts to create a culture of learning in organizations are having a broader impact. Companies that learn the fastest and adapt best to rapidly changing business environments—those with cultures of learning—outperform peer companies without learning cultures. Such cultures make learning central to everyday work life by building a community of workers with adaptive mindsets who view continuous learning as essential to organizational success.

Research from Bersin by Deloitte, a management consulting firm, examined the issue of learning cultures in detail and found that companies that effectively nurture their workforce's desire to learn are at least 30 per cent more likely to be market leaders in their industries over an extended period of time.[2]

Organizational Health

The need for L&D to evolve into Trusted Learning Advisors in the name of self-preservation isn't limited to our function or our individual selves. It's also a matter of preservation of our organizations.

Remaining order takers poses a real threat to the health of our organizations. When we routinely carry out orders for training prescribed from non-learning professionals—business leaders with good intentions but little expertise in how to conduct a needs analysis or choose the right performance improvement remedy—we almost ensure we will have to repeatedly fix the same performance problems.

Keeping L&D from using its hard-won knowledge and experience in those scenarios has huge tangible and intangible costs. There are tangible costs tied to poor design and delivery solutions when they need to be redone. The time wasted by the stakeholders, learners, and

L&D in creating poor solutions equates to significant intangible costs, not to mention burnout or reputational damage for L&D.

The failure to properly identify and fix problems the first time—resulting in poor sales performance, flawed customer service, or employee motivational issues that impact productivity, product quality or retention—also impact the bottom line and can place organizations at a competitive disadvantage against companies who have more evolved L&D functions capable of resolving problems the first time around.

I was a decade deep into my career in L&D before I realized there was a different way to do my job—let alone a better way to do it. At that point, I had been around long enough to have seen every iteration of training, and I had enough professional experience to know what it took to earn someone's trust. And yet I had never connected those pieces with the services I was providing in L&D. I was still 100 per cent an order taker, and I wasn't even aware of the concept of being a Trusted Learning Advisor.

I know I am not alone in this scenario, otherwise you wouldn't be reading this book.

In L&D we can often be unaware that we are being order takers, usually because we are in a reactive state of responding to something happening in the business at that moment. As a result of comments like "I just need it done," we end up just doing "it." From the point of view of an L&D practitioner, there is a deeply rooted mindset of, "The business said they want this, so I'm going to deliver it. I'm the order taker and I'm going to produce what I'm asked. I'm not going to push the envelope, that's what the business wants." Rather than validating the request and taking a step back to perform a needs analysis, we end up doing exactly what the business wants and we provide no additional "value add," resulting in a negative impact on the overall health of the organization and the people within it.

The Looming Skills Gap

We have shifted from a world where information was scarce and inaccessible to a world where information has become abundant and easily accessible. Knowledge was an asset for companies, but abundancy of information has made knowledge less advantageous. Knowledge is worth nothing if an individual is not able to put the knowledge into practice or does not have skills based upon that knowledge. As a result, the talent market has turned into a skills-based economy: an economy where people are valued for their skills.

A skills gap is the gap, or difference, between an organization's current capabilities and the skills it needs to meet customer demand, achieve organizational goals, and respond to market changes. A skills gap is a result of a mismatch between the skills that a potential employee can offer, and the skills being sought by the employer. Across the world, both public and private sectors are focusing on closing the gap through L&D opportunities to increase employability, because it can bring significant change to the global economy.

A project by the World Economic Forum, in collaboration with different public and private entities from around the world, reported that closing the global skills gap could add US$11.5 trillion to global GDP by 2028.[3]

A study conducted by IBM, involving more than 1,500 executives, concluded that a company's success and future is highly dependent upon its employees' skills, creativity, and agility.[4] The growth of the skills-based economy has motivated organizations to focus on recruiting people who have the ability to adapt and the aptitude to learn, thereby adding value to their company. However, more often organizations find themselves surrounded by problems because of the skill gaps existing in the markets.

Scholars such as Professor Peter Denning, L&D practitioners like John Seely Brown, Chief Scientist at Xerox and director of the Palo Alto Research Center (PARC), and institutions such as the World Economic Forum have been raising awareness for many years of a mismatch between technological advances and the existing outdated and archaic educational systems. In other words, technology evolution is outpacing the approach and speed at which we train people to respond to the related impacts.

According to Thomas and Brown in their book *A New Culture of Learning* (2011), change is happening so quickly that the value of our skills will be halved after a specific duration.[5] Denning and Brown state, "The half-life of a learned skill is 5 years—this means that much of what you learned 10 years ago is obsolete and half of what you learned 5 years ago is irrelevant."

It made my brain hurt when I initially tried to comprehend this theory. Let me explain it to you in a way that helped me understand it by applying the half-life theory to a highly in-demand technology role. In 2020 there were an estimated 25 million software developers in the world, but by 2030 the need for software developers is expected to double. This means there would be a need for 2.5 million new software developers each year until 2030. Taking the current 25 million software developers, 50 per cent will experience the half-life phenomenon with their skills.

So what?

Without additional reskilling or upskilling, only 12.5 million of those software developers will be suitable for the jobs they are needed to do by 2030. Some academics even argue that technology skills, such as the software developer, now have a half-life of three to four years, which means that even fewer will have the necessary skills for the role, and the gap will widen. The result is a deficit of qualified people to fill the necessary roles.

Personally, I find this exciting. And so should you! This is OUR opportunity to get ahead of this issue and spearhead programs to curb the internal organizational skill gaps. Our organizations aren't thinking about this. Our stakeholders don't know this is an issue. And why would they? It's not their job. This is our job, as Trusted Learning Advisors, to be forward-thinking and problem-solving before it impacts our organization. We couldn't ask for a greater opportunity to demonstrate our capabilities and our value.

The need for L&D to be a consultative business partner (Trusted Learning Advisor) is crystal clear.

In other words, our talent needs L&D. Think about that. They. Need. Us.

As a result of the ever-changing, fast-paced business environment, the shelf life of many skills, not just tech, is shrinking. With a gap in skills, organizations may not be able to grow or compete fast enough and may be ill-prepared for the future of work. Talent must remain proactive with skill development and through the L&D function, organizations must remain vigilant and provide opportunities for talent to upskill or reskill if the business hopes to remain relevant and competitive in the future.

According to a study published in 2019, 64 per cent of the 600 HR leaders surveyed said there was a skills gap in their company, up from 52 per cent in the 2018 report.[6] In 2020, 44 per cent of HR leaders reported it was more difficult to fill their skills gap than it was the previous year, and 42 per cent said the skills gap was making their company less efficient.

In LinkedIn's 2022 Workplace Learning study, 46 per cent of L&D practitioners said the skills gap had widened in their organizations, and 49 per cent of executives in the study reported being concerned that employees don't have the right skills to execute business strategy.[7]

Research from Gartner estimates that eight in 10 workers do not have the skills they need for their current or future roles. Gartner found the pandemic accelerated the need to upskill and reskill workers because it forced companies to "reimagine how, when and where work gets done."[8] Coupled with the half-life of skills in many job categories shrinking and organizations faced with needing to quickly upskill or reskill workers as their business strategies change or when digital transformation impacts the demand for new capabilities, the opportunity for L&D to take proactive action is ripe.

Effectively closing those skills gaps requires a consultative approach where L&D works closely with business leaders to identify goals and then translates them into performance improvement action plans. Although daunting, this presents a major opportunity and a call to action for us to support the business and proactively address the skill gaps.

This is the role of a Trusted Learning Advisor.

Are you excited yet?

The Talent Engagement and Retention Crisis

Consider one of the biggest problems plaguing organizations today—poor employee engagement. For the first time in more than a decade, Gallup found that the percentage of engaged workers in the US had declined in 2021. Only one-third of employees reported being engaged (34 per cent), and 16 per cent reported being actively disengaged in their work and workplace.[9]

> Studies have shown that career advancement and development opportunities serve as a meaningful purpose to employees and, when those opportunities are absent, an increase in employee disengagement can be found.[10,11] Therefore, offering employees L&D opportunities that help advance their careers and allow them to grow as individuals directly improves employee engagement.

Employee disengagement has profound costs for organizations, as unmotivated or disinterested employees often are less productive, have more performance issues, and make less discretionary effort—and are more prone to leave.

Gallup's research found employees who are not engaged cost their companies the equivalent of 18 per cent of their annual salaries. Globally about 66 per cent of the workforce is not engaged. That means in a company of 10,000 employees with an average salary of $50,000, the cost of disengagement is $60.3 million annually, according to Gallup. Globally, disengagement is costing organizations billions of dollars.

The odds of improving engagement increase when L&D are Trusted Learning Advisors.

When working as consultative business partners, Trusted Learning Advisors can use their expertise to help identify the root cause of performance or employee motivation problems. In this case, a Trusted Learning Advisor might recommend training or coaching for managers to help them better identify the emerging signs of a disengaged employee so they can intervene faster to address the situation.

Conversely, acting as an order taker gives L&D little chance to help make such a diagnosis or recommendation.

The value the L&D function can provide to the organization has been well documented in the academic literature through the years. For example, one researcher views the importance of training within the organization as an "economic necessity," further noting that "a workforce that is not trained to meet the changing skill demands of the workplace is a drag on the national economy."[12]

If the organization does not have highly skilled, effective people, the business cannot grow and be successful.

The value L&D provides is enabling leaders to focus on growing their business while L&D focuses on growing the people. Businesses evolve quickly, and the talent needs to be able to adapt quickly to those changes. L&D serves the function of supporting the talent to evolve faster to meet the needs of the changing business.

Grow your people, grow your business.

But regardless of how many studies articulate the value L&D can provide to the organization, none of the value will manifest if the stakeholders circumvent the methodology, processes, and the science of learning by dictating a solution and expecting to have it executed without due diligence. The well-documented impact of learning on engagement and organizational performance doesn't belie the urgent need for L&D to develop the skillsets necessary to evolve into Trusted Learning Advisors. A Trusted Learning Advisor does not simply take orders, but rather uses intimate knowledge of the business, listening abilities, critical thinking skills, and a knack for asking the right questions to collaborate with stakeholders in getting to the bottom of the issues, digging into the root cause, and finding the appropriate solutions.

When allowed to act as Trusted Learning Advisors, you are freed to help stakeholders consider and assess the many factors that can contribute to performance issues. The problem at hand may not be a skills-related gap, but may be caused by the work environment, for example, where an organization needs to change something about the work rather than the worker.

In some cases, training might not be the solution. Rather, it could be an ill-conceived or overcomplicated work process that keeps employees from being as productive or efficient as possible. It might be a motivation or incentivization issue, where workers don't have adequate reasons to want to do a good job. Or it could be a problem with outdated or cumbersome technology platforms that create frustration and headaches for the workforce rather than delivering new process efficiencies.

Only by building the skills necessary to evolve into Trusted Learning Advisors do you have the opportunity to make such distinctions and help your stakeholders hit the bullseye in identifying and solving the true cause of costly performance problems and delivering value.

Employee engagement issues are critical for all the above reasons, plus one more: Employee engagement issues are a precursor to employee retention issues.

2020 saw rampant workforce reductions across the United States as a result of the Covid-19 global pandemic. By April 2020, the United States reached a historic unemployment rate of 14.7 per cent—an unprecedented level since the US began collecting data in 1948.[13]

One year later, the US began to experience a different phenomenon. Rather than organizations laying off employees, employees started voluntarily leaving their organizations. According to 2022 data from the U.S. Bureau of Labor Statistics, millions of employees have quit their jobs since May 2021, a marked distinction from the mass, involuntary workforce reductions the year prior.[14] In November 2021 alone over 4.5 million employees voluntarily left their jobs, the highest monthly amount documented since record-keeping began in 2000 for voluntary resignations.

Employees are unhappy.

Although greater flexibility and an improved balance between work and personal life were cited in the initial reasons employees were leaving their jobs, as this phenomenon, known as The Great Resignation, continued on, McKinsey & Company research later identified lack of opportunity for professional career development as one of the principal reasons behind the great resignation.[15]

But this isn't new.

Multiple studies have shown that career advancement is one of the biggest factors that persuades employees to stay with a company over time. A study by the Society for Human Resource Management (SHRM) and TalentLMS found that 76 per cent of employees say they are more likely to stay with a company that offers continuous learning opportunities.[16]

A different study by the Pew Research Center found that lack of opportunity for development and career advancement was (along with inadequate pay) the top reason employees quit their jobs.[17] LinkedIn's 2022 Workplace Learning Report discovered that companies who were good at career development were able to retain employees nearly twice as long (5.4 years to 2.9 years) as those without effective employee development strategies.[18]

Many employees feel constricted and unable to advance their careers because their companies fail to provide effective L&D programs. Their workplaces had no room for personal or career growth, resulting in the employees looking elsewhere.

Employee attrition is a grave problem for organizations. Albeit not a new phenomenon, employee attrition (turnover) is a damaging and expensive part of doing business. When talent resigns, the cost to replace them can be as great as two times their salary. Aside from the recruitment and hiring costs, there is a learning curve for the new talent, sometimes lasting up to 12 months, which equates to additional loss in productivity. Those resigning tend to have institutional knowledge they've gained over their tenure, which cannot be replaced quickly. The knowledge leaves with them.

> Employee retention is recognized as an important part of overall organizational success. After all, as many say, employees are an organization's greatest asset. When organizations demonstrate they value employees by investing in their growth and development, it can result in commitment from the employee to stay with the organization.

Why should companies pay closer to attention to the employee attrition problem?

Gallup's 2019 report found that turnover costs one trillion dollars to US businesses per year.[19]

One trillion dollars.

If one single statement should be used to justify the need for the L&D function, this would be it. The issue, however, is that our function already exists in many of the companies where attrition is happening. If we, L&D, can support employee retention, but we aren't, the obvious question is: why?

The answer to where we are versus where we need to be to support the organization and attrition is summed up by three letters: TLA. Trusted Learning Advisors.

If we have ever needed a call to action, the talent crisis is it. Our talent is literally quitting because of insufficient developmental and growth opportunities, aka not enough access to us. They are not just asking for our help, they are demanding it. If it were up to us, we would have been already providing the extensive career-pathing, upskilling, reskilling, and all of the developmental opportunities needed; but it is not solely up to us.

According to a LinkedIn survey report, 94 per cent said they wouldn't resign their jobs had their employers invested in L&D.[20]

Career growth and development are increasingly significant for younger employees. Over 87 per cent of Millennials believe L&D is among the most critical aspects of company culture.[21]

70 per cent of Gen Z employees are unstimulated and want jobs that align with their passions and support professional advancement.[22]

And this is why we need to evolve into the role of Trusted Learning Advisor:

- to advocate for our talent (before they all quit)
- to proactively support our stakeholders
- to demonstrate our value proposition to the organization as a function driving employee retention

The data is clear—employees seek more opportunities and more growth, both of which are benefits of workplace L&D. We have a purpose!

Leaders looking for a tool to leverage to retain their competitive advantage and productivity through their talent are turning to us, the

L&D function. We, L&D, are an important ingredient in the solution for supporting the most important asset in organizations—talent. The missing characteristic is having L&D in the role of Trusted Learning Advisors.

EXERCISE
Your Turn

I've identified several reasons why we need to evolve. Take a few minutes and think about your own answer to this question—why do you need to evolve into a Trusted Learning Advisor? Are there other reasons you can identify, beyond what I've already shared?

Needed: Patience, Resilience, and Commitment

There is no shortage of pitfalls on the path from order taker to Trusted Learning Advisor—the biggest being time. Fortunately, in some cases, evolution takes time, and unfortunately, in other cases, evolution takes time. The L&D industry needs to evolve as quickly as, if not quicker than, the needs of our stakeholders, which means that we need to start our evolution... yesterday.

While the urge to fast-forward is understandable, it also usually dooms efforts to failure. The trust and credibility that must be built with the business during the progression can only happen with time, and by continuing to stack small wins. The stakes are high in this evolution. One misstep, one ill-conceived plan, or a rushed solution can undo months or years of work put into transforming L&D's role.

We can't simply stroll into the executive suite with a PowerPoint deck and announce we're now Trusted Learning Advisors. Those who've successfully made the progression start with realistic expectations, understand that significant change takes time, know that their skill-building must remain constant, and that it might take stakeholders saying "no" five times to get to that one "yes." But they also know it's upon that single "yes" that the foundation for change is built.

Hopefully now you have a better understanding (and might even be a bit exhausted) of the many reasons why you need to evolve. Recognizing many of those reasons yourself is probably what led you to reading this book. Thank you for sticking with me while I reinforced them, and hopefully provided data points you can leverage for your self-motivation as well as with your colleagues and stakeholders.

Now it's time to get into the heart of what it takes to be a Trusted Learning Advisor. In the next chapter, I will define the characteristics of Trusted Learning Advisors and how those traits look when applied within the realities of the workplace, with the goal of helping you to fully grasp the capabilities you'll need to develop to achieve that advisory role.

KEY POINTS

- Technology evolves. Businesses evolve. People evolve. L&D needs to evolve.
- Today there are three major drivers supporting the need for L&D to evolve into Trusted Learning Advisors:
  o our self-preservation
  o the looming skills gap
  o the talent retention crisis
- The skills and knowledge needed to perform effectively in many jobs are rapidly changing, and the trend shows no signs of slowing. In many cases that's because technology continues to advance faster than worker skills, and the accelerating digital transformation of business is shrinking the half-life of many skills.
- Employees are demanding access to our services. And if they don't receive it, they are willing to quit their jobs.
- Our evolution takes time... one day at a time, with small strides and small wins.

Endnotes

1 LinkedIn. The Transformation of L&D: Learning leads the way through the Great Reshuffle, 2022, learning.linkedin.com/content/dam/me/learning/resources/pdfs/linkedIn-learning-workplace-learning-report-2022.pdf (archived at https://perma.cc/4MNB-VKLB)

2 T Chamorro-Premuzic and J Bersin, July 12 2018. https://hbr.org/2018/07/4-ways-to-create-a-learning-culture-on-your-team (archived at https://perma.cc/7V22-PAWN)

3 World Economic Forum. Closing the Skills Gap Accelerators: Overview, www3.weforum.org/docs/WEF_Closing_the_Skills_Gap_Accelerator_1pager.pdf (archived at https://perma.cc/E5Q4-7FEX)

4 IBM. Capitalizing on Complexity: Insights from the Global Chief Executive Officer Study, 2010, www.ibm.com/downloads/cas/1VZV5X8J (archived at https://perma.cc/YF6P-SLMT)

5 D Thomas & J S Brown (2011) *A New Culture of Learning: Cultivating the imagination for a world of constant change*, Createspace Independent Publishing Platform

6 Wiley. Closing the skills gap, 2019. universityservices.wiley.com/wp-content/uploads/2019/08/201908-CSG-Report-WES-FINAL.pdf (archived at https://perma.cc/V45A-T362)

7 LinkedIn. The Transformation of L&D: Learning leads the way through the Great Reshuffle, 2022, learning.linkedin.com/content/dam/me/learning/resources/pdfs/linkedIn-learning-workplace-learning-report-2022.pdf (archived at https://perma.cc/4MNB-VKLB)

8 Gartner research report. Survey Reveals HR Leaders Number One Priority Will Be Building Critical Skills and Competencies, October 20 2021. www.gartner.com/en/newsroom/press-releases/2021-10-20-gartner-survey-reveals-hr-leaders--number-one-priorit (archived at https://perma.cc/4VT5-4553)

9 J Harter. U.S. Employee Engagement Drops for First Year in a Decade, Jan 7 2022. www.gallup.com/workplace/388481/employee-engagement-drops-first-year-decade.aspx (archived at https://perma.cc/L552-7LM5)

10 B Afrahi,, J Blenkinsopp, J C F de Arroyabe & M S Karim. Work disengagement: A review of the literature, *Human Resource Management Review*, 2022, 32 (2), 1008–22

11 A Körner, M Reitzle & R K Silbereisen,. Work-related demands and life satisfaction: The effects of engagement and disengagement among employed and long-term unemployed people, *Journal of Vocational Behavior*, 2012, 80 (1), 187–96

12 Anderson, cited in B A Altman. *The History of Workplace Learning in the United States and the Question of Control: A Selective Review of the Literature and the Implications of a Constructivist Paradigm*, 2008. Online submission.

13 U.S. Bureau of Labor Statistics. Unemployment rate rises to record high 14.7 percent in April 2020, The Economics Daily, May 13 2020, www.bls.gov/opub/ted/2020/unemployment-rate-rises-to-record-high-14-point-7-percent-in-april-2020.htm (archived at https://perma.cc/LSA7-NXQ2)

14 U.S Bureau of Labor Statistics. Number of quits at all-time high in November 2021, The Economics Daily, January 6 2022, www.bls.gov/opub/ted/2022/number-of-quits-at-all-time-high-in-november-2021.htm (archived at https://perma.cc/7VCN-82LC)

15 A De Smet, B Dowling, B Hancock & B Schaninger. The Great Attrition is making hiring harder. Are you searching the right talent pools? McKinsey Quarterly, July 13 2022, www.mckinsey.com/capabilities/people-and-organizational-performance/our-insights/the-great-attrition-is-making-hiring-harder-are-you-searching-the-right-talent-pools (archived at https://perma.cc/V9J5-9NEU)

16 Society for Human Resource Management and Talent LMS. The State of L&D in 2022, 2022, www.talentlms.com/employee-learning-and-development-stats (archived at https://perma.cc/RS2Z-AUGY)

17 K Parker and J Horowitz. Majority of workers who quit jobs in 2021 cite low pay, no opportunities for advancement, feeling disrespected, March 9 2022, Pew Research, www.pewresearch.org/short-reads/2022/03/09/majority-of-workers-who-quit-a-job-in-2021-cite-low-pay-no-opportunities-for-advancement-feeling-disrespected/ (archived at https://perma.cc/M7G7-HW6Z)

18 LinkedIn. The Transformation of L&D: Learning leads the way through the Great Reshuffle, 2022, learning.linkedin.com/content/dam/me/learning/resources/pdfs/linkedIn-learning-workplace-learning-report-2022.pdf (archived at https://perma.cc/4MNB-VKLB)

19 S McFeely and B Wigert. This Fixable Problem Costs U.S Businesses $1 Trillion, Gallup, March 13 2019, https://www.gallup.com/workplace/247391/fixable-problem-costs-businesses-trillion.aspx (archived at https://perma.cc/4K5K-638R)

20 LinkedIn Learning. L&D in a new decade: taking the strategic long view, 2020, learning.linkedin.com/content/dam/me/learning/resources/pdfs/LinkedIn-Learning-2020-Workplace-Learning-Report.pdf (archived at https://perma.cc/3XXV-A4ZZ)

21 S Thompson and Forbes Communications Council. Four Ways Companies Can Improve L&D To Increase Gen Z And Millennial Retention, Forbes, May 5 2022, www.forbes.com/sites/forbescommunicationscouncil/2022/05/05/four-ways-companies-can-improve-ld-to-increase-gen-z-and-millennial-retention/?sh=307727c743ce (archived at https://perma.cc/Z8P9-LDPE)

22 LinkedIn. Want to Retain Gen Z employees? Look to Learning, Talent Blog, May 18 2022, www.linkedin.com/business/talent/blog/learning-and-development/want-to-retain-gen-z-employees-look-to-learning (archived at https://perma.cc/MDY7-5ACU)

What Makes a Trusted Learning Advisor? 04

"*Professional trust is a process, not a state.*"

ANDY HARGREAVES

Take a moment to think about the professionals you've interacted with recently. Some doctors are warm and personable. Some are cold. Certain lawyers can be aggressive while others are flexible. Some salespeople are good at connecting with you, and others make you uncomfortable when you talk with them.

But every once in a while, you encounter someone who puts you at ease. Their presence in the room seems to be comforting even before they have done anything. They communicate with you effortlessly, almost like they're reading your mind.

You feel heard.

They seem to be able to articulate problems you didn't even know you had and offer different perspectives and solutions that work. If they have an agenda, it's not obvious. These individuals know their products or services inside and out. Their confidence is genuine. They don't have to keep telling you they're the expert; it's obvious that they are. You inherently feel they have your best interests at heart.

Your experiences with these individuals are so positive that you seek out their assistance whenever your needs cross their area of expertise. And even sometimes if it's not their area of expertise, you engage them because you know they will make the right connections for you and steer you in the right path. They take ownership, accountability, and follow through.

You can find these individuals in all walks of life. Salespeople. Customer service agents. Account managers. Financial planners. Auto mechanics. Home repair technicians. Tax preparers. Doctors. Dentists. Concierges.

It's time to add Learning & Development (L&D) practitioners to the list.

This is what I want to be: a sought-after L&D practitioner who can put stakeholders at ease because they know I am serving their best interests, I listen to them, I will deliver on my word, and they can trust me.

This should be (and hopefully will be) the aspirational goal of all L&D practitioners. For today, it starts with you setting this goal and intention for yourself.

EXERCISE
Your Turn

Take a moment and identify two examples of people in your life who you consider Trusted Advisors. What makes them Trusted Advisors?

Identifying and understanding those traits will enable you to begin to replicate them in yourself.

To start, the fundamental characteristic of being a Trusted Learning Advisor is advising, much like consulting. Consultants help people understand and solve problems by verifying assumptions and asking questions in a structured, methodological manner. Consultants are known for their expertise and grasp of subject matter; however, they are not set on one single solution or approach. Achieving consultant status means one has earned the trust and freedom to think and act at a higher level than order taker.

Being a consultant, like a Trusted Learning Advisor, is about adopting a different mindset. The consultant mindset is a frame of mind, or an approach, to the way you work towards problem solving and proactive communication. Consultants shift from jumping right to solutioning, and instead take a step back to look at problem finding and then problem solving.

Anyone can adopt a consultative mindset, focusing on how to solve problems instead of just executing the order or getting the task done. A consultant is aware that regardless of how the problem was presented, it's usually the symptom being illustrated rather than the actual problem.

A consultant is less concerned with curing the symptom than they are with curing the disease.

See the parallels?

Personal Characteristics of a Trusted Learning Advisor

John Hagel, best-selling author, career-long consultant, and founder of Deloitte's Center for the Edge research and consulting institution has long embodied the characteristics of a Trusted Advisor to serve the best interests of his clients. When I asked him how he would summarize the characteristics of Trusted Advisors, he shared the following with me:

> A Trusted Advisor will invest significant time and effort in understanding who they are serving. Trusted Advisors are determined to get to know their stakeholder and their business, and not just that person or company, but their context—it's their context that is going to shape their needs. It's investing time and effort to understand the broader network of resources that could be useful to that person or customer so that you can provide recommendations and help connect them with the most helpful resources.
>
> Trusted Advisors are flexible and adaptable. Conditions are changing at an extremely rapid rate. They need to be able to identify whether what was needed yesterday is no longer needed, understand the change, and seek out what's next. When appropriate, Trusted Advisors also need to be prepared to challenge their customers if they believe their customers are asking for the wrong product or service and suggest alternatives that might better serve the needs of their customers.
>
> Ultimately, being a Trusted Advisor is about being committed to providing value within the context of the customer you're serving.

In other words, Trusted Learning Advisors serve the best interests of their stakeholders.

Trusted Learning Advisors are:

- authentic
- proactive
- focused on continuous improvement
- able to maintain a strong personal brand
- willing to take ownership of a problem
- empathetic
- great listeners
- strong in their technical knowledge
- have deep knowledge of the business
- trustworthy
- L&D practitioners
- not after a sale
- impeccable with their words

EXERCISE
Your Turn

Take a few minutes to review this list and identify which ones you currently embody and which ones you need to cultivate further. Check in with yourself and this list on a recurring basis.

Trusted Learning Advisors Don't Sell

Trusted Learning Advisors are not trying to sell anything, including technology, but rather are impartial, unbiased, and have no ulterior motives other than ensuring the greatest outcome when recommending solutions. Trusted Learning Advisors are consummate disciplined professionals, having amassed a large toolkit filled with best practices, methodologies, frameworks, and tools to leverage that enable them to support the stakeholder.

Trusted Learning Advisors lead stakeholders to finding the necessary solution to solve their problem; they don't sell the solution.

As a result, when the overt act of selling doesn't exist, stakeholders can recognize the vibe of support, help, and curiosity which leads them to seeking our services more often.

Trusted Learning Advisors Are Impeccable With Their Words

Trusted Learning Advisors recognize that every word they speak has significant implications in their relationships with stakeholders. They are diligent and thoughtful with their communication, ensuring their messages are clear, accurate, and meaningful to avoid any ambiguity. They realize the power of integrity and consistency in their dialogues, thereby establishing a foundation of trust. The essence of their impeccability with words goes beyond mere promise-keeping; it helps in creating an atmosphere of mutual respect and open communication. Being meticulous with their words reinforces their professionalism, enhancing their reputation and cultivating solid, long-lasting relationships with stakeholders.

Stakeholders Can Spot Imposters

Developing the right capabilities and behaviors is essential because it's easy for your stakeholders to spot imitations. If you've ever talked to a so-called expert who uses the right jargon and professes to understand your problems better than you do, but after repeated exposure and questioning reveals themselves to be more about "closing the sale" than meeting your needs, you understand the dangers of acting the part without the proper foundation of skill or experience to underpin your claims of expertise.

When you encounter someone in an advisory role who quickly instills a sense of trust, confidence, and comfort, there's a feeling of instant recognition. Trusted Learning Advisors know being a Trusted Learning Advisor is an earned right, not something automatically bestowed upon them.

The following are key behaviors that separate Trusted Learning Advisors from the rest.

Being a Connector

Trusted Learning Advisors seek to connect the dots. One of the greatest value-adds that Trusted Learning Advisors can provide is to be connectors or conduits. Britney Cole, Trusted Learning Advisor and Head of the Innovation Lab at the Blanchard Company, shared key insights with me into her perspective on the way we provide value as connectors across the organization:

> One of the value propositions for Trusted Learning Advisors is looking across business verticals, brokering relationships, and making connections. In one of my previous organizations, we created most of the training content across functions, from customer care to direct sales, from field technicians to leadership development. I had visibility to every single learning initiative happening across the organization. And in true fashion, by the time the request reached me, it was already "solutioned" and my role was to fill the order.
>
> As I matured in my role, I started to notice some of the requests that came in through different business units were addressing the same need (e.g. understand product knowledge, onboarding new leaders, using same tools and systems, applying corporate policies to work, etc.). Each functional "academy" or "college" was creating their own solution and ultra-customizing it, making it unusable across functions. I realized there was an opportunity for standardization and consistency.
>
> We proposed the idea of centralizing and vetting intake requests and the training products themselves. Ultimately this saved the company a significant amount of money by reducing redundant custom content creation, created a common language amongst teams, and ultimately changed the way we operationalized L&D. As an external consultant, this focus on improving all areas of the business, even the L&D organization itself, tells your customer (whoever they are) that you care about making the best use of the investment we have. I could have just taken orders for the single customer, but instead we looked across the whole organization and changed the menu.

Our role allows us to look holistically across the organization, into silos, and through business verticals to connect problems, ideas, or people. We are in a position, as Trusted Learning Advisors, to streamline, centralize, and standardize on behalf of stakeholders where it makes sense. We can see things that others might not because of our ability to be connected throughout the organization. This is a superpower and one of our many value-added propositions.

Surprise and Delight

Years ago I was in a hotel lobby talking to a colleague about a favorite local drink in the country we were visiting. I mentioned I was disappointed the hotel bartender did not know how to make the drink. Unbeknownst to me, a hotel employee was within earshot. Two hours later I received a knock on my door. On the other side of the door stood the hotel manager and a mixologist with a tray in hand. The manager told me he had been alerted to my wish of having my drink and he was happy to be able to make it happen.

The manager and Silan, the mixologist he called to the hotel, entered my room. Now, they could have premade the drink before arriving, served the drink, and left—which was already a wonderful surprise and would have made me very happy. Instead, they did something even greater; they proceeded to make it a memorable event. They proceeded to give me a history lesson on the origin of the drink, the ingredients, and talked me through the process of making the drink.

But then they took it one step further. They had the forethought to bring enough ingredients to allow me to have hands-on practice to make the drink under their watchful eye. And, if everything they were doing to surprise and delight me wasn't already enough, they provided a performance support tool to ensure I had the tools necessary to perform successfully in the future—a printed version of the recipe! Not only did they meet an expectation I didn't know I had, but they also surpassed that expectation.

This was one of my greatest *surprise and delight* experiences; one I have never forgotten. When I think about surprising and delighting my stakeholders as their Trusted Learning Advisor, I want the outcome to include the same elated feeling I had when Silan solved my "problem." Of course, I am solving problems without the vacation atmosphere and alcohol, so it may not hit the exact same level of elation, but you get the point.

EXERCISE
Your Turn

Ask yourself this:

- What do I do to surprise and delight my stakeholder?
- How do I add unexpected value that becomes the remarkable thing that makes my stakeholder stop and think, "I didn't expect that"?

If you answered "I don't know" to these questions, this is a point of action for you. Make these reflective questions a habit to continually be asking yourself and your team members.

Think above and beyond what you are already doing and identify ways to provide that extra value-add. Proactively going above and beyond helps the stakeholder recognize you're not just an order taker providing what they asked for and nothing more.

Honesty

Being a Trusted Advisor means doing the right thing. It is giving wise counsel, good counsel; it's being selfless, not selfish. It means being honest with stakeholders. It is saying to them what learning can solve and, conversely, what it cannot solve.

In a conversation with Dr. KimArie Yowell, Rocket Central CLO and Trusted Learning Advisor, she eloquently explained her approach to the idea of honesty as an important characteristic for Trusted Learning Advisors:

> I don't ask my business partners "What training do you want?"; I ask my business "What do you want us to impact?". Often the response I receive is far greater than what L&D alone can achieve—like changing the company culture.
>
> My response to the business is to lean in, understand the challenges by asking questions, then providing insight to them on where training can support their objective and the role they have to play to impact the outcome,

through reinforcement and accountability. I explain to the business, "We are a contributor. We are an ingredient in the recipe. But we can't rest everything on what a trainer can do. We don't have a magic wand we can just wave, and everything is fixed. You play a role in this. Your leaders play a role in this. The managers play a role. We all play a role. We need to bring in multiple stakeholders if this is going to be successful."

I think that is a hard message for the business to hear. Although we aren't telling them no, we are telling them their order can't be accomplished in the manner they think it can. And I recognize not everyone is comfortable being so honest to the business. My relationship has taken time to build to that level as a Trusted Learning Advisor so I can say this to them. And because of the relationship, they know it is coming from a place of care, empathy, and positive intent. They know and understand that I see my job as a strategic enabler here to help us win. But that can't happen without honesty.

Dr. Yowell not only exemplifies honesty in her approach, but she also illustrates another characteristic necessary for Trusted Learning Advisors—being bold.

Being Bold

Being a Trusted Learning Advisor is being bold enough to say to your stakeholder, "The problem you have isn't the problem you think it is." Trusted Learning Advisors have the boldness to speak truth to power, but in a way that is safe for the stakeholder to hear. It sometimes means that you are a good bartender and therapist to whoever you're sitting across from because that is what's needed at the moment.

Trusted Learning Advisors are honest and bold connectors, with a level of expertise and partnership, who surprise and delight stakeholders.

Power Skills Needed for Trusted Learning Advisors

Power skills, often referred to as "soft skills," can be the most difficult to develop because they don't rely on memorizing facts or following a pre-defined sequence of steps—they are built by developing a deep understanding of human nature, by applying lessons learned from interacting with stakeholders, and through repeated practice, reflection, and introspection.

Power skills have taken on new importance in today's workplace—and not just among L&D practitioners. As organizations introduce more automation to the workplace and more routine tasks are taken over by technologies like artificial intelligence and robotic process automation, the power skills employees possess are what will increasingly set them apart from machines, given the human being's ability to empathize with, understand, and influence co-workers and customers.

Although we tend to focus on the power skills our learners need, many of those same skills we are advocating for apply to us. The following are the top power skills necessary to embody the behaviors of a Trusted Learning Advisor:

- curiosity
- critical thinking
- growth mindset
- agility
- empathy
- influence
- innovativation
- problem solving

Curiosity

Curiosity might strike you as an interesting choice for top billing on this list. But it belongs there because it's curiosity that encourages Trusted Learning Advisors to go above and beyond in exploring performance problems and to inquire beyond the obvious to determine what's at the root of a stakeholder's request. Curiosity begs us to ask questions, dig deeper, and seek understanding. It engages our mind and leads us into the territory of new possibilities.

Curiosity is the first real step towards change. Before you can become a Trusted Learning Advisor you have to develop a natural inclination towards questioning why things are the way they are, or how your organization's status-quo thinking and practices came to be. Curiosity inspires deeper engagement with new information. Instead of simply accepting facts and regurgitating tidbits of memorized information, curiosity allows us to take listening and learning to a deeper level.

Asking questions is one of the best tactical approaches to demonstrating and developing curiosity. As you get into the habit of asking questions whenever you receive new information, you'll naturally become better at it. By asking questions, we train our minds to seek understanding before immediately judging new information or unfamiliar people. It's through curiosity that we also can get past our own assumptions and biases, allowing us to truly understand a problem and begin to apply creative solutions that lead to business innovation and growth.

Critical Thinking

As Trusted Learning Advisors (and humans) we are inundated with information. How do we make sense of the data and information we are analyzing? How do we figure out the truth from the false, the fake from the accurate? And how do we put a lens on it so that we can have confidence that we're making decisions based on the right information? The answer: we apply critical thinking.

Critical thinking is the ability to think reasonably and objectively when analyzing information, detaching yourself from emotional responses and subjective opinions, and making intelligent decisions that yield positive solutions for stakeholders. Critical thinking helps you excel at research and be well-informed on any given topic, which is essential for a Trusted Learning Advisor.

As you approach any performance problem in your organization, there's a period of getting acquainted with the data and the facts. During this time, you may face a steep learning curve in trying to separate the facts from bias or assumptions and formulate an opinion that will guide your actions towards solving problems.

How well you make decisions based on the information available in a given timeframe is one measure of your critical thinking skills.

Those skills are vitally important as a Trusted Learning Advisor because your seat at the organizational table is predicated on solving problems for your organization. The business has a performance problem and is looking for solutions. It's your role to advocate for an effective solution and in order to do so, you need to be able to quickly assess problems and apply critical thinking to produce high-quality outcomes.

Here are some ways you can improve your critical thinking:

- Become more self-aware by thinking objectively about your skills, beliefs, morals, and ethics.
- Try to identify your biases, so you can learn to avoid them in the future.
- Try to predict how an outcome or action will affect others to come up with the best choice for that situation.
- Ask for feedback from other people, especially those with different backgrounds to your own.
- Look at the sources and citations when analyzing data.
- Think for yourself.

Growth Mindset

Psychologist Carol Dweck coined the terms "fixed mindset" and "growth mindset" to describe an individual's inclination towards learning. Those who are open to learning, as she described, have a growth mindset and those who are not open to learning have a fixed mindset.

Having a growth mindset encourages resilience in the face of change. It helps you to embrace challenges and learn from feedback. A growth mindset is pivotal to removing invisible barriers that are holding you back. A growth mindset is required to be able to successfully adopt the practices of being a lifelong learner. It is somewhere in the potential created by fostering a growth mindset and committing to lifelong learning that makes L&D more valuable than just the dollars saved from reducing turnover or increasing performance.

The growth mindset is the collective attitude we are cultivating as a Trusted Learning Advisor and a mindset we also need to have.

Adopting a growth mindset will help you continually engage with learning, keeping your skills sharp and your talent aligned with business needs.

It's important in any profession to feel like you've never truly arrived, that you don't yet know all the answers, and to focus on continuous improvement. Adopting a growth mindset will mean that you are always challenging yourself to learn, resulting in you offering the most proven, cutting-edge learning and performance improvement options to your stakeholders.

Agility

Change is constant. Our organizational, business, employee, and customer needs are constantly changing. Trusted Learning Advisors need to be able to think fast, be flexible, respond to changing needs, and be enablers of growth—all key hallmarks of agility.

Agility—the ability to understand and adapt quickly to changing situations—not only helps you pivot as your organization's business strategies may shift, but it also helps future-prepare your L&D career for whatever comes next. Change has become a constant in the business world and it's becoming increasingly important that employees at all levels adopt the right mindset and maintain a broad range of skills, knowledge, and experiences to transition into new roles or add new skillsets as needed.

Empathy

It's important to remember your stakeholders are human beings with strong emotional needs. Even in the conference room, where the topic of conversation is usually all business, your stakeholders need to feel some emotional connection to place their trust in you as an advisor. We often focus on the need to have empathy towards our learners; the same respect should be given to our stakeholders.

Stakeholder empathy is the practice of looking at the problem from the stakeholder's perspective by putting yourself in their shoes to try to understand their workflow, their challenges, their position. It means setting aside all preconceived notions, assumptions, and interpretations to understand them, where they are coming from, and how to address their feelings and concerns.

Employing empathy as a Trusted Learning Advisor is the difference between being just another expert in the room and the expert that others really trust. Empathy is the ability to understand the needs, motivations, and feelings of other people. In the case of your stakeholders, it's understanding how their success is measured on the job, what pressures and stresses they feel to deliver results, and what constraints they may be operating under.

A Trusted Learning Advisor who practices empathy is able to develop meaningful professional relationships based on human connection.

Active Listening

One hallmark characteristic of practicing empathy is the ability to actively listen. According to Dr. Ralph Nichols, "The most basic of all human needs is the need to understand and be understood. The best way to understand people is to listen to them."

As a kid, I wanted to be a detective and solve mysteries. As an adult, I've learned I can solve mysteries within organizations. Instead of being called a detective, I'm called a Trusted Learning Advisor. And like most good mysteries, we are given only a fraction of the full story when talking with our stakeholders about the "opportunity at hand." It's our job to uncover the rest of the story and doing so starts with actively listening to our stakeholders.

Active listening involves five key techniques:

1 paying attention
2 withholding judgement
3 reflecting
4 clarifying
5 summarizing

As a Trusted Learning Advisor, paying attention is not limited to what's being said; it's also paying attention to what is not being said. Our brains often process information so quickly we think we know what is about to be said or the direction where the person is headed with the conversation. To speed them along, we cut them off, attempt to finish their sentences, or start thinking about our response. Paying attention involves giving the speaker space to finish their entire thought and entire sentences without you formulating a response before they have finished. Paying attention requires being focused on the moment, being present, making eye contact (when in-person), and paying attention to both your body language and their body language.

Admittingly a challenge for most at times, it's imperative to withhold judgement or criticism when active listening—even when hearing an order from your stakeholder that you vehemently believe is the wrong approach. Given it's early in the process, we don't have all the information and need to keep our bias, preconceived notions, or prior experience out of the conversation at that moment and listen. Really listen. Actively listen.

Consider what an interaction looks like when you visit a doctor, attorney, or financial planner that you consider a Trusted Advisor. The first thing they do is listen closely as you explain your symptoms, problem, or goals. Then they ask probing questions to provide them more insight into the situation, avoiding offering up solutions until they've gathered enough background information and completed a full analysis.

Many learning practitioners are so focused on trying to solve the problem that they jump the gun and start thinking about how they're going to respond before they have heard—much less processed—what they're being told by their stakeholders. Doing so inhibits their ability to actively listen and can result in a disruption to understanding the context of what is being shared. Admittedly, this is an area I constantly need to keep in check. As soon as I hear a hint of a problem, my brain jumps right to solutioning.

Part of active listening is sitting in silence, allowing the other person to continue reflecting and sharing their thoughts. Ask the question, listen to the response. Think about what you've heard and take notes. Don't be so quick to ask your next question. Invariably, the person is going to continue talking because they don't like the silence, providing even more information—that's where all the good stuff is, the additional details you need to begin framing and solving the mystery being proposed.

Even when you think you've understood, ask open-ended, probing, and clarifying questions to encourage the stakeholder to reflect further. As Peter Drucker once said, "The most important thing in communication is hearing what isn't said."

Examples of open-ended questions include: "Say more about...", "What do you think about...?", "How might you...?", and "Can you please talk a little bit more about...?".

After active listening, Trusted Learning Advisors summarize what has been heard, giving stakeholders a chance to reflect and further clarify.

Sometimes the value of a Trusted Learning Advisor can simply be in helping stakeholders understand and organize their own thoughts through active listening.

As Trusted Learning Advisors, we follow a simple 70/20/10 communication approach:

- 70 per cent listening to understand.
- 20 per cent asking open-ended questions to ensure we understand and uncover more.
- 10 per cent summarizing what was heard for reflection and clarity.

Influence

There's no escaping the fact that being a Trusted Learning Advisor will require some convincing (aka influence). In many cases, especially in the early stages of your relationship building, you may meet resistance from stakeholders at every turn. For example, convincing stakeholders to allot additional time for needs analysis or problem investigation when they want a training solution "yesterday" will require all your powers of influence.

How you approach these scenarios makes the difference in your success as a Trusted Learning Advisor. Influence skills do not come naturally to many learning practitioners, many of whom see themselves more as educators than influencers. Yet the truth is, regardless of title or position, all of us are influencers to some degree, whether it's influencing an idea for an expanded budget, a new software platform, a new hire at work, or trying to influence against an idea you are being requested to execute.

There are three fundamental ingredients in your approach to be able to successfully influence someone:

1 logic

2 emotion

3 cooperation

Logic appeals to the human intellect. We use facts and proven successes to persuade others to see our point of view. This is why using reliable data points in your pitches can be very effective. It's why we use case studies and why we want to know more about the research behind certain claims.

Emotion, often stronger than logic, appeals to human feelings. The power of emotion to influence others is why storytelling is almost always an effective approach to introducing new information.

Cooperation is almost a synergistic approach to influence. Not only are you getting someone else to buy into your ideas, but they are helping you convince them because you are both focused on achieving a shared, mutually beneficial goal. Cooperation is one of the core fundamental aspects of being a Trusted Learning Advisor.

Having an awareness and understanding of the three components of influence can help you in discussions (or negotiations) with your stakeholders. Chapter 9 will dive much deeper into the skills and techniques you will need to overcome stakeholder resistance.

Innovation

Trusted Learning Advisors need to be creative in their thinking and think differently. Although it sounds simple in nature, the acceptance of new thinking is not easily welcomed early in our transition to Trusted Learning Advisors by our stakeholders.

"Innovation" is a multi-faceted and subjective word. If you asked 10 people to define innovation, you would receive a multitude of answers. Our stakeholders want us to be innovative, but often we miss the important task of gaining alignment and clarity with them on their definition and expectation of what innovation means to them and how they measure "being innovative."

To be innovative often refers to the act of making changes in something by introducing new methods, ideas, or products. In other words, doing something differently. In recent years, particularly for L&D, I find that innovation is largely associated with the use or implementation of technology, which can be limiting to our actual ability to be innovative. For L&D, using a different delivery approach, changing the way we measure or establish learning transfer, or conducting a design thinking initiative to uncover learner challenges fall within the definition of innovation—though our stakeholders may not overtly recognize it as such.

EXERCISE
Your Turn

Don't assume! Ask your stakeholder what "being innovative" means to them.

In Action—Changing Perception Through Innovation

The challenge of being innovative is pervasive across the L&D industry. And why wouldn't it be if stakeholders have been calling the shots for years? The order-taking mentality has stifled our ability to be innovative and, in some cases, has even created a fear of being innovative. As a result, two issues exist—L&D is not being innovative, and stakeholders don't view L&D as innovative. The two issues can exist together simultaneously or individually.

This is a challenge I've personally faced in many organizations I've worked with over the years: L&D has either not been innovative, or when it dared to try something different, it was shot down by stakeholders or not recognized as "innovative" by their definition. For one specific global Fortune 500 company, we strategically faced the lack of innovation head-on.

Let me first clarify, in this example we actually were not innovative and we were not Trusted Learning Advisors... yet. That doesn't mean we hadn't tried to be innovative. We attempted to approach solutions differently and the business rejected the ideas each time. Therefore, the team stopped thinking differently, their energy dwindled, and they shut down (burned out). We fell back in line and stayed as order takers doing exactly what the business asked. So when our stakeholders called us out for not being innovative, they were not wrong. Our response: but we are doing exactly what you ask. Their response: be innovative.

After the stakeholders told us several times that our function was not innovative, we decided to change how we approached innovation. We knew we had three challenges to overcome: the reputation of not being innovative, the fear to be innovative, and the fear of failure.

The first step was to create space where our team could prototype, test, and pilot ideas. Tapping into the power of marketing and branding, we made a strategic decision to brand our approach to innovation as an extension to our L&D group but without the immediate association by name. And there the Innovation Lab was born.

The intention of the Innovation Lab was to create a physical or virtual space where we could explore, innovate, and refine without disrupting critical day-to-day activities. The Innovation Lab allowed us to:

- respond to change quickly
- ask the right questions
- connect innovative ideas to processes
- put them in place to make those ideas happen

The Innovation Lab also helped us approach the challenge of overcoming the fear of failure. To do this, leadership reinforced that the lab was a "safe" space where our team could prototype and pilot ideas without the fear of repercussions or the fear that if ideas didn't work, it would be held against them in a punitive manner. Testing, trying, and prototyping became part of the culture and "fail" no longer had a negative connotation. For us, fail meant:

F	A	I	L
First	Attempt	In	Learning

Anything that didn't work or didn't solve the problem was still a positive data point because it moved us one step closer to identifying the right solution. Failing became celebrated as much as finding the right solution. It was a mindset shift for the team that took time to cultivate. At the same time, creating the safe space to overcome the fear of failure also provided the support mechanism to help the team reignite being innovative and thinking differently.

The Innovation Lab had a logo, tagline, and branding unto itself. By formalizing innovation, we created a systematic approach to how we thought about, structured, and presented innovative ideas.

Rather than involving the stakeholders immediately or asking for permission and risk being stifled, the team used sandbox (test) environments and mini-prototypes and pilots to test ideas and gather data points. In the past, the team had tried new ideas and approaches but without a clear structure. The strategy now was to be very prescriptive about what we were trying and why we were trying it, rather than being innovative for the sake of innovation. Each idea needed to link back to an organizational objective and clearly have a business problem identified. We tracked each idea, how it was tested, and the outcome of each test in a database. As data points were collected and ideas demonstrated positive results, we picked ideas to formalize and prepare to present to our stakeholders.

But we still had one issue to overcome—our reputation for not being innovative.

In the past, we'd taken ideas to stakeholders, presented them in an unstructured way, and were shut down. We couldn't just reach out to our stakeholders and say, "we've changed." We knew we needed to be strategic in how we approached them.

We wanted to create an experiential opportunity for our stakeholders individually to surprise and delight them. It was important that we made a curated experience all about them.

In prior situations, we had reached out to the stakeholders, sat with them in a conference room, and fought to keep their attention through PowerPoint slides. This time we took a different approach. We picked three stakeholders and identified three innovative solutions for each based on business challenges we knew existed. Each solution had an innovation lead, or host, assigned. We set up three kiosk-type stations in an empty room with a laptop and any additional tools, such as process flow charts or virtual reality googles, necessary to demonstrate the solution. Each station was focused on one business problem/innovation idea with one host assigned. Each host had created a well-crafted and rehearsed story that was relevant and contextualized to the stakeholder, including data points.

Each innovative idea was packaged and presented as a story in a standardized manner and included the following components:

- question/problem we were solving
- purpose
- benefits of the idea
- success measurement
- deployment method
- current use, if applicable
- future use

The stakeholder lab experience took 30 minutes in total: 10 minutes for each innovative solution, comprising five minutes for the host to demonstrate the innovative solution and five minutes' discussion. The only intention of the engagement was to plant seeds to help the stakeholder recognize that we understood them, understood their business, and were thinking differently about solving their problems. No permission was asked, no decisions needed to be made. The experience existed only to give individual attention to our stakeholder so they could begin to see us differently.

And it worked.

Our stakeholders told us they felt we were more focused on them, their business, and bringing ideas with intention. And it wasn't too long before our stakeholders were telling their stakeholders about the Innovation Lab and asking if they could invite others to attend. Slowly, the perception started changing and leaders at new levels were reaching out.

We continued this approach and made it part of our process to host an Innovation Lab experience at least once, if not twice, a year.

In the end, it turned out that it wasn't that our stakeholders were necessarily resistant to innovation. The root of the problem was that our L&D team did not have a structured, formalized process providing sufficient evidence of clearly articulating the "why," or taking the necessary time to identify the context, relevance, and value before we were trying to sell an idea.

The Innovation Lab was successful for a few reasons. First, it provided a structure for our team to be intentional about trying something new. We set aside time and space to take a break from our regular routines and check in to explore our creativity in a safe space. Even if we had never taken the next step, the simple act of intentional experimentation was creating a snowball effect that allowed new ideas to flow freely. We became more creative, better communicators, and better problem solvers because of this experience.

Through the Innovation Lab, our sharpened skills began to invite success. When we started coming up with really good ideas, we created experiential individualized events to communicate and inform our stakeholders of what we were doing. We invited them to see our success first-hand. We articulated the important details about why and how it worked. And we planted seeds about the value it could provide for their departments.

The Innovation Lab was a purposeful opportunity to encourage growth and new ideas. It was an exciting experiment that was creating buzz and delivering results. And our stakeholders thought so too! The change happened slowly. But it was a change. We were no longer pushing our ideas on these other departments and begging them to try new things. One by one, these stakeholders who had witnessed the success of learning in our Innovation Lab began wanting to know more and even went as far as asking to be invited to "join the fun" (their words—not mine).

We could have just sat in a conference room and talked circles for days with little success, as we had in the past. But when we showed stakeholders what innovation looked like in action—we had their attention. And it was at that moment when our expertise was highlighted by success that they could see that our relationship changed. The Innovation Lab played an important role in our stakeholders recognizing our transition into Trusted Learning Advisors.

But the biggest takeaway was that we were no longer fighting to get a seat at their table. We were making our own table and inviting them to sit with us.

EXERCISE
Your Turn

Think about your approach to innovation in your organization. Is it structured? Is it formalized? Do you have a systematic approach to linking innovation to solving stakeholder business problems? Consider how a program like the Innovation Lab could bring value to your stakeholders and help you in your evolutionary journey toward being a Trusted Learning Advisor.

Problem Solving

One of the greatest ways we add value to our stakeholders as Trusted Learning Advisors resides in the ubiquitous cycle of organizational problems. If there were not problems to be solved, the need for us would not exist. We are experts in all aspects of problems: problem finding, problem defining, and problem solving. And problems, as we know, are rarely what our stakeholders think they are.

Misdiagnosed or misunderstood problems can exacerbate company challenges and steer the team in the wrong direction. As a result, it's more difficult and costly to identify the optimal solution. Our ability to analyze and frame a problem leads to systematic problem solution and precise, effective recommendations to our stakeholders.

Trusted Learning Advisors become so good at diagnosing and solving problems that they begin to proactively find the hidden challenges (or opportunities) and are the ones to provide solutions. They are constantly scanning the environment for emerging challenges that can rack up costs, dampen sales, reduce productivity, or cause high levels of voluntary turnover.

Trusted Learning Advisors seek to get to the root cause of an issue. There are many tools and methods for doing this such as collecting and validating facts, conducting qualitative research, and obtaining and analyzing company data. The value the Trusted Learning Advisor provides during this process is the ability to remain neutral and independent, and the ability to validate and synthesize information into an informed and well-balanced discovery report.

We create more value through our ability to frame the problem than by simply reacting to the problem.

As an order taker you've likely become accustomed to either being excluded from the problem-solving process altogether, or at least functioning very reactively when you're informed of a problem that needs to be solved. As order takers it's rare we seize opportunities to solve problems outside of our silos.

That is no longer the case when you to graduate to a Trusted Learning Advisor role.

I consider myself naturally inclined to be a problem solver and it remains a skill that I must constantly practice and grow. But that's the beauty of lifelong learning—we're never at the endpoint in our journey and there is always more to learn.

Every day we are tackling dozens of inefficiencies and roadblocks that keep our businesses from achieving more through performance: downtime on production lines, warehouse picking errors, quality errors, slow response times on customer-facing communications, inefficient labor usage, or high employee turnover rates, to name a few.

Organizations use a variety of methodologies and approaches to solve these problems. For example, it wasn't long ago organizations were adopting their own version of the Six Sigma methodology, a lean manufacturing management model developed by Motorola. As one success story after another spread about how companies were adopting this model and eliminating inefficiencies to boost productivity and reach record outputs, its popularity spread like wildfire.

Six Sigma represents just one incarnation of problem-solving approaches in the business world. While approaches like Six Sigma work well for materials, in L&D we deal with people, which can require a different approach (albeit Six Sigma is a methodology you should have in your practitioner's toolkit).

We utilize problem-solving models that recognize the human element in our problems and embrace the human in our solutions. Human-centered design is an approach that provides frameworks and tools to ensure we keep the human at the forefront of our problem-solving process. Three frameworks exist within the human-centered design family and can be particularly useful for ensuring we are developing solutions with our learners in mind: design thinking, User Experience (UX) design, and Learner Experience (LX) design.

EXERCISE
Your Turn

Pop quiz! Which problem-solving methodologies are you familiar with and utilizing?

If you didn't include human-centered design in your answer, set aside time to research and develop an understanding for design thinking, UX design and LX design. To get you started, I've included a detailed review of the design thinking methodology and an L&D case study on the application of design thinking in Appendix I.

A Trusted Learning Advisor is reliable, authentic, credible, self-confident in an unassuming way, and has a genuine interest that is not self-serving. Trusted Learning Advisors put the people around them at ease. And rather than constantly thinking about how to push an agenda, Trusted Learning Advisors are simply focused on serving the needs of their stakeholders with the goal of moving the business forward.

Although it can be overwhelming and daunting to comprehend the full breadth of qualities, skills, and behaviors that define a Trusted Learning Advisor, it is integral to the success of your transformation into a Trusted Learning Advisor to understand what is expected of you. To achieve the status of Trusted Learning Advisor means you are beholden to these characteristics. Chances are you already possess many of them. Take a self-inventory to identify those you exhibit and personify, and those that need more developmental awareness.

Remember, it's a journey—not a destination.

Now that you have a deeper understanding of the skills, qualities, and behaviors that make a Trusted Learning Advisor, it's time to focus on the skills needed to ensure your stakeholder believes in you and has confidence in you, otherwise known as trust—the single component that will determine your level of success with your stakeholder.

KEY POINTS

- Transformation into a Trusted Learning Advisor requires a crystal-clear understanding of what you're moving towards. Only by first identifying and carefully defining the full complement of skills and capabilities needed as a Trusted Learning Advisor can you create an action plan to help you get there.

- Trusted Learning Advisors are honest and bold connectors, with a level of expertise and partnership, who surprise and delight stakeholders.

- Trusted Learning Advisors don't sell.

- Focus on developing mastery of these power skills:
  o curiosity
  o critical thinking
  o growth mindset
  o agility
  o empathy
  o influence
  o innovation
  o problem solving

- Human-centered design is a powerful methodology to leverage as a Trusted Learning Advisor. It's a human-centered approach that is easily applicable, flexible, and iterative, keeping the focus on the end user.

Putting the "Trust" in Trusted Learning Advisor

05

"When trust is high, the dividend you receive is like a performance multiplier, elevating and improving every dimension of your organization and your life... In a company, high trust materially improves communication, collaboration, execution, innovation, strategy, engagement, partnering, and relationships with all stakeholders."

STEPHEN COVEY

What is the most important relationship you have at work... the person you confide in and seek guidance from... the one you might consider your best friend at work? Hold on to that thought.

Now imagine you woke up today and the trust was gone. POOF! Trust no longer exists between you and this person.

Would it still be your most important relationship? Would you still confide in them and seek their guidance? Would you even want to work with them? The answer to all three is: probably not.

Although we cannot see trust and we cannot touch trust, it's all around us. It's in the brands we buy, the food we eat, the people in our lives.

Trust is the foundation of human connection.

Trust is the first step in building a relationship, both professionally and personally. Trust facilitates cooperation and engagement with your stakeholders, encouraging them to be more open with you, receptive to your ideas, and actively engaged in your process. Trust lays the foundation for collaboration and mutual understanding, while providing a framework for stability in your relationship. Trust enables you to influence your stakeholders and opens doors that may otherwise be closed.

Building, establishing, and maintaining trust is the single most important part of your journey towards becoming a Trusted Learning Advisor. After all, "trust" is the first word and the pinnacle achievement of becoming a Trusted Learning Advisor.

Building trust is a process. Sometimes it will happen quickly and other times it will take considerable nurturing. Some people give trust easily and others are more reserved. Every interaction with a stakeholder is influenced by past experiences and personal bias. Much of what goes into building trust is abstract. People skills, competence, and emotional intelligence are examples of the intangibles that factor into the equation.

Trust can be time-consuming and difficult to earn, but can very easily be lost in an instant. It is important to understand what trust is, how it works, and how you can use it to build strong professional relationships. You need to be aware of the inherent challenges in gaining the trust of your stakeholders and the importance of safeguarding that trust once earned. If you understand the components of trust and the associated behaviors, you can use that knowledge to build, and keep, the necessary trust in your relationships.

There are no shortcuts in building trust.

Defining Trust

To trust means that a belief exists in the authenticity, reliability, or believability of someone or something. Trust is a mental attitude toward the notion that someone is dependable, reliable. To be recognized as a Trusted Learning Advisor means you possess the quality of being believable or authentic and others consider you are worthy of their trust.

Trust is not automatic or immediate. Although you might have extensive knowledge in Learning & Development (L&D), this does not automatically mean your stakeholders are going to trust you. **Expertise does not equal trust.** This statement is indicative of the growing challenge educators, doctors, and scientists face with a

Figure 5.1 The Five Pillars of Trust

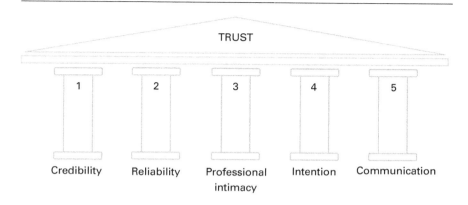

prevailing call to question their expertise. Once upon a time a prestigious university credential, fancy job title, or being in position of authority may have signaled a form of immediate trust, but the days of meritocracy appear to be long gone. Today, social media has created an environment where most determine the level of expertise (or trust) based on their personal beliefs or the echo chamber of limited ideas to which they are exposed.

Trust takes time and effort to build. But time and effort alone will not build successful trusting relationships.

Successful trusting relationships are built upon five pillars (attributes)—see Figure 5.1.

Building on the Five Pillars of Trust

The First Pillar of Trust is Credibility

The Quality of Being Believable or Worthy of Trust; Authenticity

Ask yourself: Am I believable and trustworthy? Am I authentic? Do I have a level of competency in L&D that will provide value to my stakeholders? Do I give my stakeholders the feeling of security and confidence? If not, what do I need to change?

Credibility is the foundational building block for trust. After all, if you are not believable, you will not be trusted. Would you trust someone you didn't believe? People need to know they can believe what you're telling them. Your believability comes from your character and from your competence. Your stakeholders want to know you are knowledgeable in the area where they need your expertise—which, by itself, is not enough to demonstrate credibility as a Trusted Learning Advisor.

When it comes to demonstrating your credibility, there are three key areas to focus on that will build trust in the eyes of your stakeholder: knowing your stakeholder, knowing yourself, and knowing your field of practice.

Knowing Your Stakeholder

The relationship between you and your stakeholder is so important that Chapter 6 solely focuses on providing you with the skills and strategies you need to grasp to build successful relationships with your stakeholders. The emphasis on and importance of your stakeholder relationship cannot be understated, particularly as the work you put into knowing your stakeholder's culture, language, values, objectives, and context will only strengthen your credibility.

Knowing Yourself

A study conducted by Dr. Tasha Eurich found that 95 per cent of people believe they are self-aware—but only about 10 to 15 per cent truly are.[1] The glaring difference between the two suggests we may need to spend time getting to know ourselves a little better.

The human mind is riddled with bias and defense mechanisms that serve to protect our egos. We're often unaware of our own behaviors and we continually seek feel-good releases of dopamine that come from focusing on positives. We tend to avoid dealing with negative feelings or acknowledging when our behavior or performance is lackluster or damaging to others.

We do a good job of self-praise and not such a great job of being objective. Pair this with our natural inclination to take the path of least resistance, and we're basically hardwired to find softball solutions and then pat ourselves on the back for our performance. Few are self-aware enough to even realize what is being done.

Part of your role as a Trusted Learning Advisor requires you to have difficult conversations with your stakeholders and share messages they may not want to hear (but need to hear). As I've reflected on my own behavior over the years, I found I have tried to avoid difficult conversations. To combat this issue, roleplaying, rehearsing, and practicing anticipatory thinking are tools I have learned to leverage to help me feel prepared for uncomfortable or difficult conversations.

To push past the challenge of your own resistance and build real trust based on your competence, working on self-awareness is a bridge you need to cross.

The process of getting to know yourself can be intricate. Self-assessments can be a good place to start but they can be limited by your blind spots. Reflecting on each interaction with relationships in your life, including those with your stakeholder, and identifying opportunities of improvement is a crucial activity. But it can be more useful to work with a mentor or invite diverse outside perspectives and try to identify patterns of your behavior.

Ultimately it doesn't matter if we think we are trustworthy or credible, it matters how others perceive us. Leveraging a 360-degree developmental assessment is a fantastic way to get feedback about how those around you perceive you—including the feedback from any stakeholders you are currently working with or previously worked with in this activity.

Real growth comes from being able to acknowledge your opportunities for improvement, and being willing to change. Continuous improvement and agility are two hallmarks of a Trusted Learning Advisor. The point of self-discovery is to build a relationship with yourself which leads to stronger relationships with stakeholders and the ability to grow your influence, and fuels your transformational journey to becoming a Trusted Learning Advisor.

It is not only important that your stakeholders trust you; it's also important that you trust yourself. To trust yourself, you must know yourself. If you do not trust in yourself, your decisions, or your behaviors, why would someone else trust you? Self-trust is built through your confidence. It is built through your accountability and commitment to your stakeholder, and your willingness to self-reflect and make the changes necessary to be the best advisor to your stakeholder. If you avoid self-reflection, you will struggle to build trust.

Knowing your stakeholder and knowing yourself will help you be more authentic and comfortable in building a connection through your stakeholder relationship. When your stakeholder recognizes your credibility and authenticity, it leads to greater collective decision-making which results in their buy-in for the recommendations you provide, positioning you to drive greater value for your stakeholder, business, and learners.

EXERCISE
Your Turn

Ask yourself the following questions to begin gaining deeper insight into yourself:

- How do I think about problems?
- How do I deal with other people?
- How do other people describe me?
- What are the key attributes of my personality?
- What things do I refuse to compromise on?
- What do I avoid or prefer not to do?
- Why would others trust me?
- What makes me credible?
- How can I be better?

To gain deeper insight into how others perceive you, summon the courage to ask three people you trust to answer the same questions about you. This is a great opportunity to practice active listening. Do not respond, react, or get defensive. Just listen to their perceptions. Decide which behaviors or actions you need to change to help others see you the way you see yourself.

Knowing Your Field of Practice

For your stakeholders to trust in your credibility means they are trusting in your competency as L&D practitioners. Competence is the combination of the knowledge to know what to do, the ability to do it, and the skills to apply the right solutions in the right contexts.

Competence is built with both theoretical and practical knowledge. Theoretical knowledge is based on ideas or the broader experiences of others. Theory teaches the techniques, or the reasoning-behind knowledge, without adopting a practical approach. It is possible to build a deep reservoir of knowledge without the experience of being able to use that knowledge in the real world, which is where practical knowledge becomes necessary. This is particularly valuable if you are new in your career as an L&D practitioner and gaining knowledge.

Practical knowledge is the knowledge or experience you acquire through hands-on experiences. Practical knowledge is gained through real-life endeavors and tasks by doing things. For example, reading about design thinking will provide you with an understanding of "what" it is. But until you have hands-on experience with a design thinking initiative, you won't have practice at applying what you have learned, otherwise known as practical experience. Theoretical knowledge is gained, for example, by reading a book, whereas practical knowledge is gained by hands-on doing. You are building your theoretical knowledge at this exact moment!

Both theoretical and practical knowledge and experience are necessary for L&D practitioners.

Competence is a key part of building trust that falls within credibility. After the first impression fades your competence becomes the focal point.

The funny thing about competence is that you are often unaware of your own incompetence. While others can sometimes see it glaringly, you don't know what you don't know. And even when you do become aware of it, there are four different levels of competence to be aware of:

1 unconscious incompetence

2 conscious incompetence

3 conscious competence

4 unconscious competence

You start out blissfully ignorant of what you don't know. For example, for years I was an order taker without understanding the full implications of that role. Similarly, the L&D industry has long operated as order takers and were proud to be doing it because it never occurred to most practitioners there was a different way to be.

This *unconscious incompetence* is where you begin when you don't know what you don't know. You don't have any awareness of your incompetence.

Things changed for me one day when I read a book (maybe you can relate?). Later I listened to an L&D practitioner talk about ways the industry needed to change and the science of learning. And then there were podcasts, articles, and additional content I consumed. As my brain began to connect the dots, I realized there was more to my work and something greater I could be achieving that I didn't even know existed.

I began to see my career field in a different light. At this point I had no idea how to be different. But I was starting to become aware of a new possibility. I was now *consciously incompetent*. Now I knew there were things I didn't know. I didn't have a formal name for it yet, but I knew I didn't know how to be a Trusted Learning Advisor. But I was beginning to see a better way to serve my organization.

As my views changed, my career trajectory began to change with it.

I had lit a fire that I didn't even know needed to be burning. I was curious, driven, and now I was growing an insatiable appetite for learning. It was all new. Growing up I struggled with learning. And now suddenly I was championing this idea of continuous lifelong learning, growing myself and my team. And little by little, I developed *conscious competence* at the early stages of being a well-rounded L&D practitioner.

Within a few years, I had completed a Master's degree and applied for a doctoral program in education. I immersed myself in learning about learning and human behavior. I studied trends in learning and sought out plenty of new opportunities to build skills. I understood that full competence doesn't come from reading a textbook or listening to the anecdotes of a college professor. It doesn't come from heartfelt chats with trusted mentors. While all these things contribute to building competence, real competence isn't one-dimensional.

Competence is the combination of the knowledge to know what to do, the ability to do it, and the skills to apply the right solutions in the right contexts. It takes all three—knowledge, skills, and ability—to be competent.

As I embraced learning, I steadily became consciously competent in many areas. I began to build knowledge in L&D beyond simply doing a job. I had years of experience suddenly framed in a new context with this knowledge. My confidence grew and my abilities developed. Pretty soon I wasn't just an order taker anymore. I was a competent practitioner working my way toward becoming a Trusted Learning Advisor.

Conscious competence means you have certain knowledge, skills, and abilities but that you are very calculated in applying that competence in the real world. When you use learning theories to design training, it's a very conscious effort to transfer the knowledge of those theories into the practice of creating impactful learning experiences.

But as you practice more, things become second nature and you settle into your expertise. This level of *unconscious competence* is fluid. You make competent decisions effortlessly based on your knowledge and experience without consciously connecting those dots. It's more like second nature. It becomes a natural execution requiring no thought—like breathing. It's a way of being. This level of competence is where Trusted Learning Advisors need to be. It's where I strive to be.

Keep in mind there is a distinction between competence and over-confidence. The balancing act to take into consideration is that when you believe you are competent and do not manage your behavior, it can lead to overconfidence in competence, resulting in telling the stakeholder what to do. You are not in the business of telling your stakeholders what to do. You are in the business of leading your stakeholders to the right solution.

Chapter 7 will cover in-depth guidance and support on crafting your L&D practitioner skills.

I've spent a few pages highlighting the importance of understanding competency for a reason—competency is necessary to build credibility. And credibility, as you might recall, is the First Pillar of Trust.

The Second Pillar of Trust is Reliability

Being Depended On for Accuracy, Honesty, or Achievement

Ask yourself: Can my stakeholders depend on me? Do I deliver consistently? Am I reliable to myself?

Being reliable means that you are showing up and delivering consistently.

To receive trust from others, they need to know that you will do what you say you will do—always. Your stakeholders are looking at whether you are consistent with your words and actions and if you can follow through with what you've said you can and will do.

Being consistent and predictable in your behavior helps to establish that you are reliable. When others know what to expect from you, they will be more willing to put their trust in you.

Lauren Weinstein, a learning professional at Microsoft and Trusted Learning Advisor, shared with me that reliability is one of the most important aspects of building trust where she maintains constant focus:

> I look for every opportunity to show that I care and follow through on my commitments. I make sure that my stakeholders know they can rely on me and that I will deliver what I promise. Doing so helps to build trust and develop my relationship with stakeholders. But this is a learned behavior.
>
> In my first job out of college as an analyst at Accenture, I was eager to succeed in my role. I was so focused on saying "yes" and trying to

keep my stakeholders happy that I ended up making commitments about deadlines that I couldn't always keep.

I remember my boss telling me at one point that I needed to under-promise and over-deliver. I took this feedback to heart and started building in extra time when setting project completion timelines. Soon, I was surprising and delighting stakeholders by delivering on time and surpassing their expectations.

Trust is built with the actions, words, and behaviors that happen in between what you say you are going to deliver and what you actually deliver. Trustworthiness depends on ensuring stakeholders can count on you and be confident that your words are not empty promises.

But if you want to prove reliability and let others know you act on your intentions, you must first understand whether you can rely on yourself. It is not enough to want to do something and leave stakeholders in awe of your abilities, but rather actually being able to accomplish it.

The solid path to being a reliable Trusted Learning Advisor is knowing you can undoubtedly deliver what you have promised. That sense of clarity and confidence comes from delving into details, asking relevant questions, and understanding whether an undertaking aligns with your experiences, skills, interests, and potential.

Be sure you can meet your stakeholders' expectations and requirements. If you're insecure about whether you have what it takes to complete something in the expected time, communicate it. Ask for clarity. Seek support.

It is always better and more honest to admit something is outside your expertise field than to delve into a project you can't complete, ending up with your promises falling short and losing trust.

Know your strengths, possibilities, and limits.

You can only practice reliability and turn it into your forte if you consistently follow through on your word and take on challenges you can tackle. Others should never doubt whether you can handle something because you know your boundaries and never stretch too far beyond them without the necessary support in place.

The best way to be a reliable person is to be good at setting and enforcing boundaries. When you have good boundaries, you're better equipped to handle the obligations that you've committed to—and you are more easily able to recognize when to say no.

The Third Pillar of Trust is Professional Intimacy

Close Association With, Deep Understanding Of, or an Affinity for Someone

Ask yourself: Do I know anything personal about my stakeholder? Have I invested any time in getting to know my stakeholder on a deeper level? Does my stakeholder know anything personal about me? Am I willing to be vulnerable with my stakeholder?

Many overlook the importance of establishing and nurturing a positive connection with stakeholders. They direct their effort toward the practical side of the job and forget that we are all humans, filled with feelings and emotions. It is human nature for people to crave those they interact with to acknowledge them as unique individuals with feelings, hopes, and struggles.

Nurturing intimacy will create a feeling of safety, encouraging other to communicate openly with you if they know they will encounter understanding and friendliness. As a Trusted Learning Advisor, your role is not to judge, be detached, or appear transactional.

Instead, you should care about your stakeholders and all intricacies that affect their communication style, requirements, and standards. Doing so shows you're an empathetic human and that you care about them and the impact of your work and methods.

Your L&D coworkers, clients, and business partners should feel at ease with you and enjoy engaging with you, which helps drive better results and lasting connections. Moreover, authentic and innovative programs and solutions emerge much more often from human-centric collaborations when people feel safe enough to express themselves and their opinions.

Building healthy professional relationships takes a lot of the same communication skills as any personal relationship. You need empathy, discretion, emotional intelligence, and active listening skills. When tensions rise, you need to be skilled at managing emotions. Focus on reading the emotional cues of those around you to energize your relationships and give others what they need to place their trust in you.

Check out Chapter 6 to dive deeper into developing professional intimacy.

The Fourth Pillar of Trust is Intentions

Desired Result, Purpose, or Motives

Ask yourself: Am I clear about my intentions with my stakeholders? Do I have ulterior motives? Am I clear about my stakeholders' intentions? What's my "why?" What's my stakeholder's "why?"

Understanding and reflecting on why you do what you do is an important part of understanding your intentions and motivations.

Everyone forms relationships with some sort of purpose, intention, motivation. Healthy relationships are formed with the intention of social bonding and mutual success. Less healthy relationships are formed with the intention of self-orientation. Sometimes in business, people strike up alliances because they get personal gain from it. Trustworthy people steer clear of pushing agendas or selling.

It's very common that your own intentions will creep into your activities and interactions with your stakeholders, consciously or unconsciously. Put forth the effort to check in with yourself and be as conscious as possible about your motives or purpose by discussing them with your stakeholders.

Leave no place for assumptions, miscommunication, and misalignment. Your stakeholders, clients, and colleagues should know what to expect from you and how you turn strategies and methods into tangible work. Let fairness, ethics, and strong principles drive your collaboration with others.

Respect your stakeholders, understand how you can help them, and use your abilities to materialize their concepts and ideas. But, also, be forthright with yourself about why you're doing something. Understand what you want to accomplish and whether that aligns with what you said to your stakeholders.

Hidden and ill intentions are always more transparent than you might assume, resulting in broken alliances and damaged reputations.

Let others know the details and ensure you share the same objectives and approach.

Doing so helps establish connections on stable foundations and build trust. Without that straightforwardness and commitment to bond for a connected cause, you will struggle to earn their trust.

The Fifth Pillar of Trust is Communication

Being Bold, Provocative, Honest, Transparent

Ask yourself: Am I willing to tell my stakeholder the truth, even if it's uncomfortable? Am I willing to challenge my stakeholder's requests in a respectful manner when I do not believe it is in their best interest?

Without communication, Trusted Learning Advisors cannot be understood and cannot understand stakeholders. Communication is required to be able to articulate stakeholder problems and offer solutions. Communication skills go a long way toward determining how your stakeholders view you and whether they perceive you as a credible and trustworthy partner.

Good communicators are much more than articulate, well-spoken individuals. They are approachable, offering gentleness around awkward subjects—such as when suggesting to stakeholders that training might not be the right solution to their challenge—in a way that puts everyone around them at ease.

Even if you doubt your stakeholder will agree with your suggestion or approach, it's your job and duty to be authentic and tell the truth. Stakeholders might not always know what direction is best for the project—they are relying on you to guide them. This is why they trust you.

Trusted Advisors value and exhibit honesty, understanding even the smallest white lie or broken promise can undermine confidence and damage relationships with stakeholders. Don't steer away from challenging conversations or fear that saying something might cause you to lose a client. It is always better to have someone disagree with you and walk away than be dissatisfied and cancel collaboration later because of lack of communication. That's where your expertise and knowledge enter the picture. Discuss the details and reveal all intricacies that play a role in your collaboration and future strategies.

Trustworthy people are transparent. They keep the lines of communication open to minimize confusion interfering with progress. They always ask for feedback—and not just once. They continually check in with stakeholders and say what needs to be said. Trustworthy people are masterful at having difficult conversations. They don't avoid conflict and they are able to prioritize constructive progress over feelings but with respect. Avoid sugar-coating or concealing some parts because you think that would make it easier for a stakeholder to agree.

Strong communicators set realistic expectations and aren't afraid to be assertive when they have strong convictions. Stakeholders know exactly what to expect when interacting with this type of individual, making it easier to let their guard down and begin building trust.

Stakeholders must know where they always stand with you and be able to trust your words and intentions. Give them no reason to doubt or question your collaboration.

Through communication, you create genuine dialogue, providing structure to conversations that allow stakeholders to maintain focus. This includes the ability to design meetings, convene the right people, and manage healthy conversations. In conversations, Trusted Learning Advisors identify and give voice to the value-added activities and discussions that wouldn't routinely or naturally occur in organizations by creating a degree of safety which increases the likelihood that all ideas get expressed, heard, and given fair evaluation. Doing so reduces the effect of positional authority, or intentional biases, agendas, or individual incentives.

In other words, communication creates trust.

Spotting Signs of Mistrust

When you're trying to establish trust in a relationship, it's important to understand the different ways people might signal or express their mistrust (or lack of trust) in you. As you begin to recognize these familiar actions and phrases, you can identify opportunities to take a step back and work on those relationships so you can build trust and approach them again in the future.

Few people will come right out and say, "I don't trust you." Instead, they disguise their lack of trust in different ways.

Tell-tale signs that trust is lacking in your relationship with your stakeholder:

- Excluding you from important meetings or conversations.

- Withholding or resistant to sharing information with you.

- Responding to you with hostility, resistance, or an endless barrage of questions.

- Appearing guarded and unfriendly, such as crossing their arms, avoiding eye contact, or seeming preoccupied while speaking with you.

- Quickly giving you a dismissive, default excuse that lets them off the hook or being noncommittal.

If it feels like you are trudging through mud to get small things done, it's likely that you need to spend more time cultivating trust and less time pushing your agenda.

REMEMBER

The process of building trust is deeply involved, requires commitment, and takes time. After all, it's not just one or two components to monitor and master to build trust, there are five:

1 credibility
2 reliability
3 professional intimacy
4 intention
5 communication

Being a trustworthy person takes discipline. Building trust can be challenging and you may potentially find yourself wanting to compromise along the way to take, what may seem at the time, the "easier position."

Hold your integrity.

The short-term discomfort you might feel with a difficult conversation is minimal compared to the laborious, and sometimes impossible, task of repairing a relationship where the trust has been broken.

The higher the level of trust in the room, the more innovative, dynamic, creative, agile, and effective the relationship will be.

Make trust a priority. Your future as a Trusted Learning Advisor depends on it.

Now that you have a deeper understanding of the importance of trust and the ways to build trust, the next chapter will cover the cornerstone to your success as a Trusted Learning Advisor and the key to getting the real work accomplished—relationships. With trust and a healthy relationship, there is nothing you can't accomplish with your stakeholder.

FIVE PILLARS OF TRUST RECAP

- **Trust requires credibility**. To be credible means you are competent. Competence is the combination of the knowledge to know what to do, the ability to do it, and the skills to apply the right solutions in the right contexts. It takes all three—knowledge, skills, and ability—to be competent. Building trust around competence means we have experience and skills in the area of practice where the stakeholder needs our support.

- **Trust requires reliability**. Individuals who appear to have a strong moral or ethical compass are viewed as consistent and reliable. They use intrinsic motivation to guide their actions rather than bending to the whims of those who influence them. This predictability in their behavior makes it easier to give them trust.

- **Trust requires professional intimacy**. When we consider someone trustworthy, it activates our pleasure and reward center in the brain, allowing us to attach positive emotional connections to that relationship. Individuals who are warm and empathetic have an easier time earning the trust of others compared to those who are cold and emotionally distant.

- **Trust requires intention**. Being intentional involves understanding the reasons behind your actions, understanding your "why." Intention means understanding what you want to accomplish and whether that aligns with what you said to your stakeholders. Hidden and ill intentions are always more transparent than you might assume, resulting in broken alliances and damaged reputations. Let others know the details and ensure you share the same objectives and approach.

- **Trust requires communication**. Honesty and transparency are symbiotic components for trustworthy communication. An honest person who is reluctant to share the reasons behind their actions will always invite more questions than an honest person who reads like an open book. How you deliver the truth makes all the difference in how the message is received by those around you. To earn trust, you need to be transparent about your goals and what you hope to achieve with every recommendation you provide to your stakeholder.

KEY POINTS

- Building trust with stakeholders is arguably the most important predictor of your success as a Trusted Learning Advisor.

- Trust is difficult to earn and easy to lose. But understanding the psychology behind human behavior greatly increases the odds that you will build and maintain trust.

- Because humans are feelings-first creatures, it's important to understand the power of emotion in building trust. One self-serving agenda, for example, can shake or shatter trust forever.

- Trustworthiness has five key components: credibility, reliability, professional intimacy, intention, and communication.

- Three factors accelerate trust-building: developing an intimate understanding of your business partners, knowing yourself, and acquiring deep knowledge of the L&D field.

- High-level communication skills separate pretenders from contenders among Trusted Learning Advisors. Developing and continually honing these skills determines whether business partners will view you as a trusted and credible authority on performance improvement issues.

Endnote

1 T Eurich (2017) *Insight: Why we're not as self-aware as we think, and how seeing ourselves clearly helps us succeed at work and in life,* Currency

Building Relationships: Your Bedrock for Success

06

"Individually we are one drop, but together we are an ocean."

RYUNOSUKE SATORO

Imagine for a minute you've had a very stressful week. Your domestic life isn't as solid as you would like and although you try not to let it spill over into work, it's nearly impossible to separate the emotions between your work and home lives these days. To make matters worse, you are working on a stakeholder project nearing its deadline but unfortunately, it's hit a snag. As of right now, you are certain you are not going to meet your deadline and there is a chance it's going to also cause the project to go over budget.

You are exhausted both physical and emotionally, and if someone looks at you the wrong way right now, you fear you may simply crumble to the floor. Although you and your team have given it your best, there are circumstances outside of your control that will hinder the project and you know what needs to happen next—inform your stakeholders the timeline will not be met, and additional costs may be incurred.

Here's where a decision needs to be made. This project has two stakeholders—Darla, a newly appointed stakeholder who you've only had a limited number of conversations with, who you know nothing personal about, and who also has a reputation for making people cry when her expectations are not met (and by the way, this behavior is never acceptable); and Lucinda, a stakeholder you've completed several successful projects for, laughed through your first yoga class together, and hugged when she experienced the loss of her mother.

Do you:

1 Tell no one and hope it solves itself before someone finds out?

2 Talk with Darla and Lucinda together?

3 Talk to Darla first?

4 Talk to Lucinda first?

5 Start looking for another job?

Two of these we can immediately discard. If you aren't sure which two, it's 1 and 5. As a Trusted Learning Advisor, you know you must communicate to your stakeholders regarding any impacts to the projects. And as for 5—you are a Trusted Learning Advisor, you don't just quit when it gets difficult. You navigate through it. It's your job and your commitment to steer your stakeholders through those rough waters—that's what makes you a Trusted Learning Advisor.

This leaves you with 2, 3 and 4.

If you were feeling solid and stable, it might not be a difficult decision. You could talk to your stakeholders together, but knowing how Darla reacts, it might be more strategic to speak with them separately to have an ally on your side and feel you have support in the room. You could talk with Darla first and use tools such as roleplaying your conversation to feel prepared and hopefully reduce her reactions. But that doesn't feel possible today. After all, today you are feeling especially human. Therefore, I imagine you would pick 4 and speak with Lucinda first. Me too.

But why are we both picking 4?

It's simple—you have a relationship with Lucinda. And relationships are how you get the help and support you need to get the work done. Relationships help you feel connected, like you are a part of something. And relationships are critical in our personal and professional lives.

Relationships are the connection, association, or involvement you have with other people.

Your area of opportunity, of course, is to build a relationship with Darla—but you can start that journey another day when you feel more grounded. For today, you start with Lucinda. You know she will treat you with kindness and empathy because you have a relationship with her. You trust her and she trusts you. You know she sees you as a partner and not just a provider. She is your ally. It doesn't mean she will be thrilled to hear there's a delay and possible cost increase, but it means she will listen and work with you. Chances are, she would even be willing to join you for the conversation with Darla to lend her support for the approved timeline extension.

This is the power of relationships and the ingredient for how the real work gets done.

The cornerstone to your success as a Trusted Learning Advisor can be found within the relationships you cultivate across the organization—starting with your stakeholder. The stronger the relationship, the greater the chances are for joint success. Although it is possible to produce successful outcomes and initiatives without strong relationships, the chances of success increase exponentially for you, your learners, your stakeholders, and the organization as your relationship with your stakeholder becomes solidified. Building a relationship with your stakeholder can positively influence outcomes in ways that cannot always be accomplished by only following plans and processes—without the human connection.

When trust exists and relationships are built, it is easier for people to work together more efficiently and effectively. Investing time and energy into building a relationship with your stakeholder can:

- reduce project risks by increasing confidence and minimizing project uncertainty
- help overcome unexpected challenges that may arise
- help cut through corporate bureaucracy
- increase the project delivery time by speeding up problem solving and supporting a more holistic decision-making process
- improve your reputation as a Trusted Learning Advisor by having your stakeholder act as your champion and advocate in the organization
- increase the chances for future work

Although there are many facets and characteristics for relationship building, as Trusted Learning Advisors, I find there are five components necessary to include that will set you and your stakeholder up for success:

1 understanding stakeholders and their business
2 identifying the baseline of the stakeholder relationship
3 establishing your credibility
4 speaking their language
5 setting clear expectations

Understanding Stakeholders

Keep in mind, stakeholders are people too... and possibly they are also order takers. Building the relationship with your stakeholder starts with having empathy and understanding them as people.

Britney Cole, Trusted Learning Advisor and Head of the Innovation Lab at the Blanchard Company, shared key insights into her perspective on the importance of understanding the stakeholder in the relationship-building process:

> If you want to build a solid relationship with your stakeholder, put yourself in their shoes. Maybe they're coming to the Learning & Development (L&D) team because it's the only influence they have to effect change. All they can do is build a course or fill a perceived knowledge gap with content. Perhaps they know the system is broken or the policies are inherently unmotivating, and the only thing they can do is increase knowledge or build skills, which can perhaps demonstrate workarounds to the broken system, or be transparent that the policies often have a reverse effect.
>
> Instead of immediately pointing out that training might not be the answer (which it never solely is anyway), ask yourself these two questions: "How can I best meet the root cause of this need with what I have?", and "How can I make them look like the hero?"
>
> It's not about your desire to build an awesome course or use a simulation or create a chatbot. It's about helping your stakeholder

provide as much value as they can to their job and be the hero of their story. When you flip the script and think about others, practicing what we call servant leadership, you might see the solution a bit differently. When you focus on helping your client achieve their outcomes the best way you can (which might be through a course, performance support, email campaigns, or learning pathways), you become a true leader and an advocate of why we are all here in the first place.

Our industry needs champions—those who believe that the work we do matters to others. These people will be the ones who change the hearts and minds and recognize L&D as Trusted Learning Advisors.

Your goal is to make your stakeholders look good and to help them win with their stakeholders, which ultimately supports the learners and the organization. Helping them win starts by understanding them, their perspective, and their "why." The following are examples of general questions you can ask stakeholders to start to understand their "why":

- How are they impacted by the project?
- What's their current opinion of your L&D function and/or the project?
- What are their interests in the project?
- What are three key challenges their business is facing?

This type of initial information gathering is important as it gives you insight into their position regarding your relationship or project (i.e. supportive, conditional, neutral, undecided). Having this understanding will help you learn what is important to your stakeholder, allowing you to adjust your messaging to meet their needs or wants.

As Britney so beautifully posed it—how can you make your stakeholder look like the hero? Stakeholders know that if you can make the problem better in their environment, they'll do better. Keep in mind your stakeholders have self-interest that the order they are giving has a successful outcome. They want you to be successful; they are not intentionally setting you up to fail.

> **REMEMBER**
>
> Seek to understand your stakeholder. Exploring their self-interest is one
> approach to understanding their "why" and persuading them toward a
> different approach if their order is not in their best interest.

Understanding the Stakeholder's Business

Being confident and competent at your craft is imperative. But no
matter how confident or competent you are, if you do not understand
your stakeholder's business, your L&D credibility of competence
flies out the window. As a result of not knowing the business or being
able to speak their language, it turns into the business telling you
what to do.

When you don't understand the business, this is an all-too-com-
mon order you may receive as a result: "You don't understand my
business—this is what we need. Please get it done."

It's hard to argue against that statement when it's true if you do
not understand their business.

A common thought or response is, "Well, the business must know
best since they are the business; they know what they need."

No, not true—at least not the part about the business knowing
what they need. It's true they might know what they want, but not
what they need when it comes to L&D services. After all, they are the
experts at their business, and you are (or should be) the experts at
L&D. But your role as a Trusted Learning Advisor requires that you
are competent about their business too.

Steps to Understand the Business

It's your role as a Trusted Learning Advisor to make a concentrated
effort to know the business and know what the business and stakeholders are trying to accomplish. This can be achieved in several
ways:

- Conduct qualitative research (or just talk) with leaders, managers, and frontline workers in the business to understand what they do, why they do it, their challenges, and their culture.
- Find out their quarterly and yearly strategic goals.
- Understand how the business plays a larger role within the organization and ties to the overall organizational goals.
- Identify their three- to five-year strategy.
- Use data from research firms to gather insights on the market direction for the stakholder's industry.
- Understand the competitive landscape the business is facing and research three competitor companies to understand their strategies, challenges, and growth plans.
- Identify the value of the company in the marketplace (market capitalization), year-to-date volume of sales, and % of growth the last four quarters.
- Be able to articulate the top three challenges the business is currently facing.
- Understand the landscape of the previous three years for the business, including challenges and successes.

EXERCISE
Your Turn

Each of the items above should be included in your initial relationship-building activities with your stakeholders and repeated at least on a yearly basis. If you have not executed any of these activities in your existing stakeholder relationships, make this a priority in the next 30 days.

If you know the direction where the stakeholders and business want to go, you can proactively look for shifts in the trends and support them through it. It is easy to ignore the bigger picture of what is happening in the business. But, by being aware of their needs, by talking to them about how they're seeing the future, how they're seeing their strategies play out, and what worries them enables us to influence more effectively and gain credibility.

By paying close attention to the business, such as knowing the market cap today, volume of sales, or % of growth last quarter, you can speak the same language and demonstrate your credibility—these are indicators that L&D doesn't often pay attention to but are important to the business. Knowing this information and using it in discussions with the business and tying solutions back to these data points and organizational goals enables you to demonstrate you have an understanding of the business, which results in a great opportunity for influence and establishing credibility.

Do your homework. Research the business, their challenges, competitors, and future landscape. Help them see the value you can provide as their Trusted Learning Advisor who understands their business.

Identify the Baseline

Building a relationship with your stakeholder starts with evaluating the type of relationship that currently exists with the stakeholder. Some stakeholders are looking for L&D to be somewhere between transactional and transformational. They look to and value the core skill development because it's something tangible that can benefit their business.

Other stakeholders may struggle to see the value of L&D and view it more as a check-the-box activity, as something you "need to accomplish." And then there is another group of stakeholders who may view training as the magic elixir to fix all organizational problems.

Figure 6.1   Finding the baseline

| ← | -5 | -4 | -3 | -2 | -1 | IDEAL POINT | 1 | 2 | 3 | 4 | 5 | → |

| Merely a check-the-box activity | | Values the tangible benefit to business | | Magic elixir to fix all problems |

Where does your stakeholder sit with regard to their beliefs or expectations from L&D? If you don't know the answer to this question, have a discussion with your stakeholder.

Equally as important as understanding what your stakeholder thinks about L&D is understanding their personal experience with learning. As you are building your relationship, ask your stakeholder about their most impactful learning experience... ever. See what comes to mind for them. Was it a grade school teacher who gave them support and encouragement? Was it a class in college that turned them onto a career path? Or maybe it was a program delivered through the workplace? With some stakeholders I've uncovered they could not recall any impactful experiences. Others I've spoken with spoke fondly of formative education and some had positive workplace learning experiences. But there are a few who shared a contempt for workplace learning programs altogether.

A simple question exploring the stakeholder's personal relationship with learning can give you insight into their experience and their potential bias.

ASK YOURSELF

What type of relationship do I have my stakeholders today? Is this the type of relationship that will lead both of us to success or are there areas of the relationship I need to improve?

Establish Your Credibility

Establishing your credibility is the First Pillar of Trust (but you already know this, assuming you read Chapter 5). But credibility also plays a key role in building relationships. Trusted Learning Advisors seek to establish credibility with the stakeholder from the initial point of contact.

Often our job titles in L&D only provide relevancy or signaling to those inside the learning industry. Titles such as Solutions Architect, Performance Consultant, or Instructional Designer do not demonstrate the breadth of our capabilities. Other Trusted Advisors such as doctors, lawyers, and dentists have their credentials framed on a wall to illustrate or signal their expertise to their stakeholders. It's not as easy for us to use labels and vocabulary to provide clear signaling on our capabilities and credentials.

EXERCISE
Your Turn

Ensure your stakeholder knows your background; don't shy away from your expertise. Unless you want to carry around your framed degrees and certifications, consider sharing your bio or resume with your stakeholder for review.

Another way you can help to establish credibility is by demonstrating the breadth of relevant experience you have and the resources that you have the capability to access (e.g. industry case studies, academic research). One of the most important aspects when establishing your credibility is focusing on points that are relevant, contextualized, and practical specifically for your stakeholder.

Relevancy and context are not only important to make learning stick; they are also important when building relationships. Tell the stories relevant to your stakeholders, using case studies or scenarios which have been applied elsewhere in a similar situation or context and framing the story so they understand how it could apply in their context and the value they would receive.

Several years ago, I was in a business review meeting with an important stakeholder where this advice was not followed. Our team spent time researching new learning technology in the marketplace and we identified two new tools to demonstrate to our stakeholder in the meeting. At the end of the demo, the stakeholder turned to me and asked, "What exactly does this have to do with our work? How is this going to help us execute our strategy?"

We froze.

We were so excited to show that our team was forward thinking and cutting edge that we forgot to do the most important part of the preparation—identify what problem it would solve for the client, making it relevant and contextualized for them. The result was a very dissatisfied client saying to us, "Don't ever bring me a show-and-tell idea without the business case for how it would apply to me."

This was a basic foundational relationship-building mistake on our part—one I would never repeat again.

Context is everything… for your learners and for your stakeholders. As one chief financial officer once told me, "I have too many fires at my feet to care about learning. In theory I know it's valuable and necessary but it's not my job to know about it. It's L&D's job to help me care by helping me understand how it's going to solve my problems."

Keep the stakeholder and business in the forefront of thought when identifying experience, stories, data, or any other activity to build credibility. Incorporating keywords associated with your stakeholder's business and minimizing the amount of custom L&D language can help to establish context and relevancy, also known as speaking their language.

Speak Their Language

Every company has its own corporate language that is comprised of words or visuals to communicate internally and externally. Beyond the corporate language, there may be other dialects spoken internally depending on the business unit or stakeholder. Acronyms and lexicons are two common examples found within organizations that deliver meaning to those who can interpret and understand them. The L&D industry is no different. We have our own language, our own acronyms, our own measurement practices, theories, and models.

In order to build relationships, you must communicate in a way that your stakeholders understand. Part of your responsibility as a Trusted Learning Advisor is to understand and utilize the language of your stakeholders. When you speak to your stakeholders (or anyone outside of L&D), it's important to make the discussion relevant and contextualized for them; make it easy to understand.

You do this by speaking your stakeholder's language, using their terminology, and their vernacular. This means that you need to do some prework before engaging in conversations.

EXERCISE
Your Turn

To understand their language, you should:

- ask for any acronyms list, definition documents, or vocabulary decoders
- review the mission, vision, and/or values for the business
- read the corporate filings, shareholder, or CEO letters or reports
- talk to frontline workers to identify any important dos/don'ts for culture and language
- If you have not taken this action yet, set a goal to have this completed in the next 30 days.

If all else fails with the above suggestions, look at industry-related terms found on Google. This will give you a basic foundational awareness on key terms.

Understanding corporate language and culture is an important part of building relationships and setting you up for success. Recently a company asked me to help them with a design thinking initiative. In my initial discovery of the culture and language in the company, I learned the organizational culture had an adverse reaction to the use of the word "empathy." Leadership had shied away from using the word, unofficially saying they considered it "too touchy feely and didn't fit within our culture." As my work was around design thinking, and the first phase of design thinking is "empathy," this could have posed a significant problem. Had I not discovered the resistance to the word up-front, I would have spent time launching change management initiatives to educate on the empathy phase in design thinking, going against the grain of the organizational culture. Instead, I switched the word "empathy" for "understanding" and was able to deliver the same message but with vocabulary that suited their culture.

Another example can be found with the words "prototype," "pilot," and "experiment"—three words with similar meaning, but the usage may result in different outcomes. I've worked in a culture where "prototype" and "pilot" were not commonly understood or made people uncomfortable, given the more formalized context the words usually represent. In that case, using "experiment" might drive a more meaningful connection with the stakeholder. "Can we try a small experiment to see if the proposed solution might have an impact? I think that might give us some real insights into what's really going on. Would you mind if we went and tried this?"

REMEMBER

You must understand the business and your stakeholders by using their vocabulary to make your solutions make sense to them. It's not their job to understand learning theory principles or your vocabulary, but it is your job to understand theirs and help the business make sense of what you are proposing to solve their problems.

Set Clear Expectations

Wouldn't it be great if every new person you met or relationship you were building came with a set of instructions or a decoder for their personality, their likes, and their dislikes? Good news! It can. You just need to provide the necessary framework to uncover the information you need. It's as simple as that.

It could be argued that the most important part of building relationships, particularly with stakeholders, is setting expectations. Without a level of clarity about the needs and expectations of your stakeholders, you don't know what they want, need, or expect from you, making it virtually impossible to manage their expectations. As a result, you run the risk of not being able to deliver on your value proposition to your stakeholder and to the organization.

One tool I use when I am building a relationship with a stakeholder is a *Partner Expectation & Commitment Charter*. A Partner Expectation & Commitment Charter is a template you create that you and the stakeholder fill out. The output of the information will help you and your stakeholder articulate what you expect to receive as a partner, but also what you expect to be giving, including insights that would be valuable for how you work together and how you communicate.

It's an opportunity for you to share what is important to you and what your stakeholder should know about you. For example, I am very accessible. I send emails at all hours of the day/week, but this might not be appropriate to my stakeholder. However, I can never be reached immediately by a phone call; I never have my phone ringer turned on. But I am always accessible through text messaging and will respond usually within 20 minutes. This type of information is important for stakeholders to know as we are building our relationship. This activity helps to build trust and accountability as you are agreeing to be held to your commitment and expectations.

There is no right or wrong way to conduct a Partner Expectation & Commitment Charter practice. Typically, I will have the questions outlined and my answers defined before proposing the activity with the stakeholder. It can be as formal as putting together a presentation or as informal as a discussion where the questions serve as the framework. Regardless of the process, it's important to document the answers for both you and your stakeholders. This document should serve as an organic tool leveraged throughout your relationship to refer to during times of miscommunication, frustration, or evolution of expectations.

The following are examples of questions to consider including when developing your Partner Expectation & Commitment Charter:

- What is the preferred method, channel, and cadence of communication?
- How often will you meet?
- What matters most to your stakeholder and you in this relationship?
- What's worked well in previous stakeholder relationships they've had? What would they do differently this time?
- How do they define and measure the success of the relationship?
- How do they prefer to handle conflict?
- What can I expect of you?
- What commitments can you make to me?
- What should I know about you and the way you work?

EXERCISE
Your Turn

If you do not already have an existing document like the Partner Expectation & Commitment Charter, start one. Today! To help get you started, I created a template charter in Appendix VI that you can use. Feel free to edit it as you see fit.

Once you've decided on the questions for you and your stakeholder, share the template with your stakeholder and give them the opportunity to add any additional questions and then time to complete it individually while you also do the same. Once completed, come together, review your responses, and set yourselves up for a successful working relationship based on clear expectations and commitments.

Properly identifying, documenting, and managing stakeholder expectations will strengthen the relationship, build trust, and increase the chances of value-driven output to the organization.

Nurturing the Relationship

After the relationship has been formed and expectations have been set, relationships take ongoing nurturing (or maintenance). I follow three strategies to continue fostering the growth and health of the relationship:

1 Stay connected with your stakeholder.

2 Ask your stakeholder for feedback.

3 Share your successes.

Stay Connected

Establishing the communication cadence is agreed upon and set in your Partner Expectation & Commitment Charter. However, that doesn't preclude you from taking extra steps to stay connected with your stakeholders. Connecting with your stakeholders on a recurring basis and driving the conversation is an important element in building a successful relationship.

The key is doing so proactively rather than reactively. I aim to stay one step ahead of my stakeholder with the way I manage the relationship in hopes they never need to reach out to me first. My philosophy is if my stakeholder needed to reach out to me first, I failed. Based on a recurring meeting or my proactivity with staying close to my stakeholder, my goal is to know when to reach out to them first.

It's important to meet with your stakeholder on a recurring and ongoing basis. At minimum, you should be meeting with your stakeholder once a quarter for a Quarterly Review meeting to plan the next three months and review the last three months. This allows you to stay connected and current.

Approach these conversations as opportunities to demonstrate you are their partner—which means significant planning needs to go into these meetings. For example, showing up to the meeting and simply asking, "What do you need?" is how an order taker would approach the meeting—immediately closing the door for consultative discussions. Leading with the question, "What do you need?" sets the tone that you are waiting for the business to tell you something or to give you that next order. Instead, ask, "What is keeping you up at night? What are some of the business problems or challenges happening right now?"

But before meeting with your stakeholder, it's critical that you put in time and effort to plan for your stakeholder review by identifying challenges the business might be having. Before meeting, take time to gather the following data points:

- Review market research on the competitive landscape and see what challenges other businesses might be having that could be relevant.

- Review industry research material.

- Read latest reports from Gallup, World Economic Forum, McKinsey Global Institute or Bersin, and identify the changing landscape of the business or what type of roles or skills are changing or may be needed in the near future for the business.

- Talk to other people in the line of business to get their perspective and insight, including frontline workers.

Doing the research and arming yourself with information that could be valuable to your stakeholder or, at minimum, indicates you are knowledgeable on their business, helps to reinforce your commitment to understanding them and their business. As a Trusted Learning Advisor, you should already have a data-driven, informed point of view on what is being discussed in your meetings with stakeholders.

The conversation is not only about receiving new information but an opportunity for you to validate information you've gathered and leveraging it in the conversation. Your goal is to leave the meeting with alignment from your stakeholder, having demonstrated to them that you have done your homework and are well-versed in their business and the industry.

EXERCISE
Your Turn

During each meeting with your stakeholder, take the lead. Provide a clear agenda prior to the meeting and consider including a few thought-provoking questions to prime your stakeholder:

- What are the current priorities for your line of business?
- What are the current challenges your business is facing?
- How do you see your business shifting in the next four quarters?

Doing so will help your stakeholder see you are focusing on them and their business and lead to a stronger relationship.

Ask for Feedback

Do you know what your stakeholder truly thinks about L&D, your team, or the support you provide? Do you know what the opportunities for improvements are or the current strengths from the stakeholder's perspective? The answer is probably "no," unless you are a mind reader or, more plausibly, you have asked for feedback.

Feedback typically happens as a result of or reaction to an action or behavior. Feedback is valuable information that can improve organizational performance, increase engagement, and strengthen relationships.

Feedback can also be difficult to hear if you are not mentally prepared for it. That's why there is great power in asking for feedback proactively—putting you in control over the conversation. And while I've not encountered a stakeholder who doesn't love to give feedback, proactively asking for it and driving the questions can offer your stakeholder a clearer direction regarding the type of feedback to give.

EXERCISE
Your Turn

If you have not asked for feedback from your stakeholder in the last 30 days, make this an action item to complete within the next 30 days.
   When asking for feedback:

- Be clear that you are asking for their honest thoughts.
- Focus on what needs improvement, rather than what went wrong.
- Start with generalized questions:
  o "How would you rate the success of our relationship?"
  o "What's working/not working for you?"
  o "What feedback can you give me?"
- Only then move to explicit and specific questions:
  o "What would you like to see done differently moving forward?"
  o "What could I do to make Project X even more successful?"

Your only role is to listen rather than judge the feedback. Becoming defensive is a natural instinct, but doing so signals to the stakeholder you are not listening, and it will make them less likely to be honest with you or provide feedback in the future.

In my organizations, our team meets with our stakeholders on a quarterly recurring basis. We also conduct an annual survey with a wider audience to provide us with documented feedback while collecting data to measure the NPS (net promoter score) of our relationship, quality of service, and areas of opportunity.

Feedback does not always need to be gathered at specific timed intervals. Make asking for feedback part of your normal cadence, creating space and time for your stakeholder to feel comfortable to share with you at any point. By limiting the feedback to once per quarter, you may miss out on learning important information in a timely manner if you have set expectations to only ask once every three months.

Following this type of practice has consistently surprised me by uncovering successes and challenges from the stakeholder's point of view that we were unaware of, and also has changed the way stakeholders view L&D. Asking for feedback demonstrates you value the input of your stakeholder, ultimately improving the output of the value you provide. Creating space for your stakeholder to provide you with feedback is a mechanism to help foster a constructive and productive long-term relationship.

Share Your Successes

If I asked you to tell me about your successes or your team's successes, you could probably identify several within the last few months. But chances are, there are many other successes you are forgetting or successes you aren't aware of happening within your team.

One of my best practices is keeping a running list of every "win'" or success our team has. Each quarter I compile the list and then I pass it to my team to add to it—no win is too small to be captured. We then make two versions—one for our internal L&D team, and one for our stakeholders. The L&D version will be the exhaustive list, but the stakeholder version will be more condensed and strategic, considering not every win is relevant to them. We use this list to craft our story, our value-add, and we bring it into a meeting with our stakeholders to discuss.

It's important to share your successes with your stakeholders, not just successes you believe occurred with that business partner, but any successes aligned with organizational or business goals reinforcing your broader reach. The approach, however, should be prescriptive. Rather than sending an email with ROI or evaluation data saying "Hey, look how great we are" (particularly since that type of data is usually more meaningful to us than to them), include successes in your discussions with your stakeholders as a dialogue—not as a "report out." Depending on how often you meet, consider it a topic to cover quarterly. Sometimes what you believe is a success might not translate to the business. Share with them where you think you are adding value and ask for their feedback. Do they see the examples you identified as value or benefit to the business? Are there other areas of value they see based on work you or your team have provided? It's a great way to start a conversation to identify other ways you can provide value as well as offering them an opportunity to provide feedback and input on what you've captured as value-add.

Ultimately, the underlined intention of your being a Trusted Learning Advisor is to always be providing value. Value can sometimes be subjective. Having this type of review discussion helps to reveal any subjectivity by either party.

EXERCISE
Your Turn

If you don't already have this as a habit, start documenting each success for you and your team members. Review the comprehensive list internally to celebrate with your team each quarter.

Next, make a version for your stakeholder (possibly not every win will be applicable/relevant for your stakeholder), and share it with them in-person (live or virtual). Use the list to drive a discussion and identify any additions or deletions from the stakeholder's point of view.

Another way to share your successes is to create more formalized case studies based on your work, demonstrating the problem, the approach, the solution, and the business impact. This can be used both internally with your stakeholders and leadership, but also externally in learning conferences, academic journals, or industry publications to help reinforce your credibility.

Case studies serve as fantastic opportunities to bring your team together on the effort, helping them step back to see the overall picture of the value they are providing and the impact they have on the business. Often our teams are only exposed to one sliver of the project. Formalizing case studies helps them to see the full story.

Case studies can also be used as part of the submission process for L&D industry awards, such as the Brandon Hall Excellence Awards, the Chief Learning Officer Learning in Practice Awards, Training Industry's Top Training Companies, and the Association for Talent Development (ATD) awards. Submitting for, and hopefully winning, awards is a great way to follow a formalized and structured approach for creating the narrative for your successful L&D projects. The output of the award submission or case studies can also serve as great tools for new joiners on the L&D team and/or for new stakeholders as a means of demonstrating your credibility and a concise story on the value you provide.

Stakeholder relationships not only take time to build, but they also take time for ongoing maintenance. To continue fostering the growth and health of the relationship, stay connected with your stakeholder, ask your stakeholder for feedback on a recurring basis, and share your successes with your stakeholder to ensure they recognize the value-add being captured across the organization.

Building Relationships Across the Organization

Relationships with our stakeholders, albeit critically important, are not the only relationships necessary for your success as a Trusted Learning Advisor. You should be cultivating relationships across all verticals and at all levels of the organization—from C-Suite to the frontline worker. It starts first with figuring out who your allies are across the functions.

Identify Your Champions

In my experience, I've found it's easy to identify the detractors of L&D across the organization; those are the ones who yell loudest about their disdain for the learning platforms or unhappiness with being taken away from work for a required training or frustration with the annual cycle of compliance training. On the opposite end of the spectrum, there are undoubtably a few gems who recognize the value of learning and who are supportive of your efforts. These are your allies—find them!

Through the years one of the most important strategies I've used in establishing our team as Trusted Learning Advisors is identifying supporters, change agents, advocates, champions, cheerleaders, or any other type of supportive classification you'd like to use—these are people throughout the organization/business units that are supportive of L&D. Identifying these individuals provides you an opportunity to have a direct hotline into the business to understand challenges and feedback from frontline workers. This group can be a superpower. It provides several opportunities:

1 Access to frontline workers to learn first-hand the challenges they and the business may be facing.

2 Access to learners on the receiving end of training, allowing you to follow up and gather feedback from them.

3 An opportunity to market learning initiatives with people who can share the message with others.

4 Access to employees who can participate in focus groups to help you gain insights into their shared perspective on learning initiatives and organizational challenges.

In one of my prior organizations, champions were one of the most important ingredients in our evolution to being recognized as Trusted Learning Advisors. Like many training organizations, our team was focused on churning out the necessary training and "launching" it. The problem was, launching the training consisted of activating it in the LMS, putting it into a course catalog, and sending out an email. We didn't consider that the LMS email was one of 100 emails learners received within a week, and most were being ignored or deleted when they came from our group.

Once we started conducting qualitative research with our learners to find out ways we could support them, we would hear requests over and over again for training that already existed. Exasperated, we would tell them, "Didn't you know that was already available? We launched that six months ago!" They would stare blankly back, asking, "How would I know that?"

It was then we realized we were failing at marketing the training. Like many, we assumed, "If we build it, they will come." It turned out to be more, "If we build it, we will send out an email and hopefully someone will open it or proactively search for it in the catalog." Understandably, neither happened.

Recognizing we needed to keep a direct line with the frontline talent, I asked my team a provocative question—"Who likes us?" My thought was if everyone had five friends in the business, we could easily identify 150–200 people who could be our lifeline to the frontline. They could help us get the word out when new initiatives were launched. Of course, we had to figure out the motivation for them, what was in it for them—just because they liked us didn't mean they'd want us to be bothering them.

After an initial one-on-one dialogue with the identified champions to ensure they were on board (and yes, it was a lot of phone calls), we set up a virtual voluntary quarterly meeting where all champions were invited. We would spend the first few minutes reviewing the programs that launched in the quarter and targeted programs for the next quarter. But, more importantly, we spent the majority of the meeting asking thought-provoking questions and just listening.

The WIIFM (what's in it for me) for the champions was the direct line to us, L&D, and the opportunity to give us feedback on training initiatives they completed or feedback on challenges, problems, or opportunities occurring within the business where training might be able to support. A good percentage of the information we uncovered could not be solved by L&D; the issues were operational, systems, or cultural. However, we could listen, and we could bring the new data points back to our stakeholders proactively, which demonstrated we were directly connected to the frontline and had firsthand knowledge of brewing organizational issues. Our stakeholders were elated when we presented the findings we uncovered, linking it back to measurable data points connected to their business goals.

Find that early adopter, bring them into the pilot or prototype, listen to their feedback, get their buy-in and engagement and, assuming it's successful, you have a supporter. And then you have a plausible internal story to tell.

EXERCISE
Your Turn

In the next 30 days, identify five champions across your organization who are supportive of L&D. Ask your colleagues to do the same. Schedule a voluntary virtual "open office hours" type session to:

- share the programs launched in the past six months
- share the programs being launched in the next six months
- capture feedback on business challenges
- capture feedback on their L&D experience
- identify what else they might need to be successful in their job

---

Establish an L&D Advisory Committee

One of the many value propositions of being a Trusted Learning Advisor is our ability to act as connective tissue throughout the organization. We can see across organizational verticals, into business units, and through silos. Rather than perpetuating a separatist mindset for our stakeholders, one practice you can consider is to break down the walls and create opportunities to bring together stakeholders from multiple levels across the organization in a think tank-type initiative to establish an "L&D advisory committee." This is in quotes because you should name the group whatever is appropriate for your organization, leveraging vocabulary that coincides with your company culture.

The members of the committee are your key business stakeholders as well as carefully curated other stakeholders. For example, I include my key stakeholders, one or two strategically selected leaders in the organization (possibly C-suite), one or two frontline L&D members who are integrated in the business, and one or two frontline managers from the business (usually picked or approved by the stakeholder of the business).

At different times, I include strategically appointed guest attendees based on the meeting topic, ranging from other internal leaders to external L&D practitioners/leaders from outside organizations. Bringing in outside resources enables you to showcase ideas and best practices being applied elsewhere.

> It's important to ensure diversity among those included, to minimize the struggle of unintentional power dynamics.

The purpose of this committee is to review the landscape across the business and have an ongoing dialogue about business goals, challenges, and ways in which L&D can support. Doing so creates space for you to be seen as a Trusted Learning Advisor and lead a discussion on critical workplace learning or performance needs and industry trends. It's an opportunity for you to share your ideas, feedback, success stories, and industry or organizational research. It's a chance to demonstrate your value; you are not just a siloed business line partner, but integrated across the organization as the connective tissue.

This board does not meet often, maybe twice a year, but it's a carefully orchestrated event where you are the conductor. This is an opportunity for you to shine by driving the conversation: sharing research on industry trends, articulating business challenges, demonstrating ways L&D can support and is supporting the organization, and presenting opportunities that may exist across business units, thinking holistically.

This is where you demonstrate the art of systems thinking and your value as a Trusted Learning Advisor. *This is your table*, and you are inviting others to sit with you to have an equitable and inclusive strategic conversation—led by you.

You may not be ready for this… yet. L&D advisory committees will place you in an elevated spotlight, which means you need to have your craft well perfected. I recommend having this be an action you take well after you've read, understood, and applied the practices in this book. If you were considering a four-year L&D strategy, I would place this sometime in year three. Trying to execute this committee too soon can set you back in your pursuit to be recognized as a Trusted Learning Advisor.

Relationships, like trust, take time and effort. Where many go wrong with relationship building is trying to rush it and not making enough time to build the relationship. It's in the small moments where the work really occurs, like utilizing the time before a meeting starts for small talk or taking time to check in on your stakeholder if they have not been feeling well. These actions show that you are paying attention and that you care, and both go a long way in building relationships.

The ultimate outcome from the relationship between Trusted Learning Advisor and stakeholder is one of partnership and collaboration. As you are building your relationship with your stakeholder, create guidelines, rules of engagement, and an expectations charter for how you and your stakeholder will work together.

Having a solid, healthy, and successful relationship sets you, your stakeholders, and your organization up for success. It enables you to have a conversation where the stakeholder can say what they are trying to solve for and accomplish, and you can give insight and feedback on the best ways you can support the goals while setting expectations for realistic outcomes.

Together you come out of the meetings with something beautiful—unified goals and next steps. The stakeholder goes back to focus on their area, and you go back and work with your team on delivering the necessary outcome. Time isn't being wasted, and you are able to accomplish what the organization has engaged you to do—drive value and provide impact.

As a Trusted Learning Advisor and steward for the company, building relationships with stakeholders is simply good for business.

Although relationships and trust are pivotal for success with your stakeholders, neither can happen until you have established yourself as a true L&D practitioner. The next chapter will address the skills you need and the approach to take when crafting your L&D practitioner skills.

KEY POINTS

- Relationships are the cornerstone of your success as a Trusted Learning Advisor.
- When trust exists and relationships are built, it is easier for people to work together more efficiently and effectively.
- Core components necessary to build relationships include:
  o understanding the business
  o determining the baseline of your relationship
  o establishing your credibility
  o speaking their language
  o setting clear expectations and measurable goals
- To ensure alignment, create a Partner Expectation & Commitment Charter.
- Relationships need to be nurtured and maintained—this is accomplished with ongoing communication with stakeholders.
- Core components necessary to maintain relationships include:
  o asking for feedback
  o staying connected
  o sharing successes
- As the connective tissue, you need to build relationships across organizational verticals.
- Two approaches to building relationships across the organization include:
  o identifying champions
  o establishing an L&D advisory committee (but not before you are ready)

Crafting L&D Practitioner Skills

"Beware of unearned wisdom"

CARL JUNG

To be a Trusted Learning Advisor requires a foundation of knowledge in Learning & Development (L&D) and a breadth of practical experience.

Disclaimer: After 24 years' experience in the industry, two masters' degrees, and a doctorate, I can unequivocally state I do not know everything about the field of L&D. Sometimes I feel like I have just scratched the surface. It would be impossible to distill down everything I've learned and everything you need to know about being an L&D practitioner into one single book, much less one single chapter. There are numerous books already written on this topic—check out Appendix III for some of my favorite recommended L&D industry books. This chapter is not intended to be an exhaustive manifesto, but rather highlights some of the important tools, skills, and practices that should be in focus for you on your journey as an L&D practitioner.

Also, this chapter may not directly apply to you if you have 10+ years' experience in the field of L&D. That's not to say you won't learn anything here—I'm certain you will—but I cover some very fundamental information on building practitioner skills that every L&D practitioner should know.

"Trusted Advisor" is a ubiquitous term that can apply to anyone, regardless of their role or function. Everyone has the opportunity to develop the skills of, and should strive to be, a Trusted Advisor. But this book is not focusing on everyone. This book is focused on elevating one field—L&D—into Trusted *Learning* Advisors. The road toward your evolution as a Trusted Learning Advisor starts with the continuous development of your practitioner skills in the field of L&D.

Practitioners don't just "happen"—they are made.

A practitioner is someone who is qualified and actively engaged in their field of work. Being "qualified" in the L&D industry can be subjective. Although certifications and standardizations exist, they are not required, which means we need to hold ourselves accountable to understand the breadth of the science of learning and put it into practice.

Active engagement is more than simply "doing your job." In L&D, active engagement means investing time and understanding into the academic and theoretical side of learning—not just the application. It means focusing on learning frameworks, theories, and strategies on an ongoing basis to ensure your training is grounded in research-based learning methodologies.

Loren Sanders, Trusted Learning Advisor and CVS learning leader, shared with me her "a-ha" moment when realizing early in her career there is more to the craft of L&D than most initially realize.

> My eyes really started to open about the complexities and scientific nature of our industry when I realized that the people who had gone through the training that we were providing weren't being successful in their job. Although we were providing all the information they needed, they weren't really learning. I kept seeing that happen, and I couldn't figure out why.
>
> I started researching, "Why can't people do their job when they have the information," and I realized the difference between learning and knowledge. Just telling somebody something or just giving them something to read doesn't make them able to perform successfully.
>
> I started learning and understanding there was a science to this! There were methods and practices that created better approaches and ways to make learning stick. It reminds me of the adage: telling isn't training. There is a craft and science behind what we do. It is our responsibility to put in the work to develop our practitioner skills to ensure we are setting our learners up for success.

As a Trusted Learning Advisor, your skills, knowledge, and intelligence in the field of L&D equate to your competence (or expertise). And having our stakeholders believe we are competent in L&D is required before we can establish ourselves as being credible Trusted Learning Advisors.

If you are early in your career (less than five to seven years in the industry) you are not an expert yet, nor should you be expected to be an expert at this point. Expertise takes time and experience. But, by reading this book, and investing in yourself to build up your skillset, you are on the path toward expertise, at least on the theoretical side.

I personally view "expertise" as a journey, not a destination, and a bit subjective. Although I have over 20 years' experience in the industry, I am constantly still learning and seeking new information and knowledge. Although I have a wealth of experience, knowledge, and tools in my toolkit gathered over the years, each new problem or opportunity posed has a unique set of variables to be uncovered and explored. I call myself a "learn it all" rather than a "know it all." I don't know it all… but I can learn it all.

The Problem with L&D

The L&D industry is welcoming, with minimal barriers for entry. It is inclusive, accepting, and non-discriminatory. Anyone can call themselves an L&D practitioner without needing to provide any validating credentials. This is both an opportunity and a challenge, having an impact on the professionalism of our industry.

The sense of being a professional, where the art of practice is important, is being missed; the L&D industry left it behind somewhere. L&D is a profession. As such, we need to act with professionalism and work toward ensuring others treat us as professionals. Like with trust, it's earned—not demanded.

If you were a physiotherapist, and a patient said to you, "My shoulder hurts. There is no need to explore anything else, I know what it is. Just fix my shoulder," you are going to do what? Take a magic wand, touch their shoulder, and send them on their way?

Probably not. You would explore and analyze other parts of the body to diagnose the issue and possibly uncover the fact that the issue is not the shoulder at all but rather an issue elsewhere being reflected in the shoulder. And how do you develop these skills necessary to know how, where, and what to analyze?

Education. Practice. Experience.

A physiotherapist doesn't just call themselves a professional immediately when they enter their line of work. They spend years training and developing themselves into a professional through practice. You learn to be a physiotherapist by countless hours of working with different people to understand their individual nuances. You learn by doing, by exploring, not by someone telling you the diagnosis. The bad shoulder is the starting point; that's the symptom.

I recognize if the industry were not so accepting, I would not have the career I do today. But I can't help but wonder the unintentional damage I caused along the way given I transitioned into L&D with no competency in the field. I spent the good part of eight years "existing" in my job without understanding or applying the science of learning, focusing on evidence-based measurement, understanding performance support, or building relationships with stakeholders or learners. I didn't have the theoretical knowledge and I was slow to build the practical knowledge.

I'm not the only one. I know many who are actively looking toward the L&D industry for their next career because with a little bit of self-marketing, a sprinkle of certifications, and a touch of experience with the right software or LMS, they can classify themselves as an L&D practitioner. This "opportunity" is part of what holds our industry back from the migratory transition from being treated as order takers to being recognized as Trusted Learning Advisors.

Although I support equal opportunity and access (again, recognizing I wouldn't have the career I do without it), I only wish a welcome kit was provided for those transitioning to help them develop the professional skills necessary to support the learners, stakeholders, and themselves.

> **ASK YOURSELF**
>
> What have I done recently to develop my L&D practitioner skills? How am I staying relevant and educated?

Our industry focuses on the development of skills for our learners, but it first needs to start with our own. As L&D practitioners, our learning should never stop (hence the moniker "lifelong learners").

The opportunity not only exists for those wanting to transition into careers in the field of L&D, but also with those of us who have been in the industry for years—we need to keep our craft and skills fresh.

In 2004 I trained for the New York City marathon. Training was grueling and rigorous, but I was dedicated and determined to see it through. And I did. It was both my first and last marathon. But, as any of you marathon runners would know, just because I practiced and trained 20 years ago for a marathon and ran it, does not mean I can call myself a marathon runner today (nor can I actually run a marathon today).

The same applies as L&D practitioners. Just because you studied instructional design or were a teacher 20 years ago, that does not mean you are finished. Our careers are like non-stop conveyer belts. You have to keep moving and growing no matter what stage of your career you are in. Our field, like our learners, is constantly evolving and we must stay in front of it to keep our skills fresh, relevant, and demonstrate our expertise, which requires us to develop deep knowledge.

Measuring Your Competency

As L&D practitioners, we know the importance of assessing our learners. We measure the knowledge they have before the initiative, measure what they learned during the initiative, and measure the transfer of learning back to their role once the initiative is completed. Without measurement, we don't know the level of impact.

If you can't measure it, you can't understand it.
If you can't understand it, you can't control it.
If you can't control it, you can't improve it.
—James Harrington

Assessment and measurement does not only apply to our learners; it applies to ourselves. Part of crafting your L&D practitioner skills is to know your level of comprehension, competency, and where you need to focus for development. L&D practitioners need to reflect and assess themselves, their strengths, and their areas for improvement.

ASK YOURSELF

When was the last time you assessed your L&D competencies?

The L&D Maturity Level Model

Each of you is on a unique path and journey in your evolution as a practitioner. But to figure out where you need to go, you must first figure out where you are today.

I have created an L&D Maturity Level Model (Figure 7.1) to serve as a general framework with which you can evaluate your path toward being a Trusted Learning Advisor. Think of the model as stages. Take a moment and reflect on where you land on the model today.

Level 1: Training Administration

It's important to recognize not everyone is beginning the journey to Trusted Learning Advisor from the same place. For example, if your day-to-day job still looks much like an administrative role, plucking predesigned compliance training content off the shelf and designing or delivering learning to the exact specs prescribed by your business partners, you're probably at the first stage of L&D maturity, *Training Administrator*.

Figure 7.1   The L&D Maturity Level Model

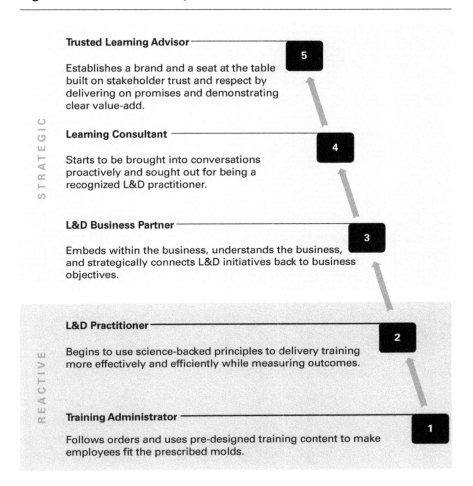

At this maturity level, you are operationally focused, needs analysis is often nonexistent, and you are not positioned to provide collaborative consulting with business partners. This is a purely an order taker function.

Much learning conducted at this level is reactionary and often untethered to strategic objectives. A culture of learning has yet to be established. At this first maturity level—especially if you're part of a smaller company or start-up—you also may be significantly under-resourced and under-staffed.

Level 2: L&D Practitioner

As you gain experience and hone your craft, you begin to gradually move from the purely reactive, ordertaking stage to the second stage of maturity, the *L&D Practitioner*. In this stage you begin to make more science-based recommendations that better shape learning initiatives in the organization.

Instead of only funneling employees through standardized or prescribed training programs, you start to offer more personalized development plans and may start using practices like spatial learning and repetition, blended learning, performance support tools, and follow-up coaching to make learning stick. The function also may purchase technologies like a learning management system (LMS) or a learning experience platform (LXP).

In this level, greater understanding and emphasis is placed on measuring learning outcomes by providing more credible evidence of training transfer and learning application on the job.

All of these changes begin to slowly shift how the business perceives the L&D function.

Level 3: L&D Business Partner

The transition between being a reactive participant and a proactive, strategic learning leader begins to accelerate at this third level. Here, as an *L&D Business Partner*, you begin to embed yourself into the business. You attend more meetings with stakeholders, become more aware of initiatives that will require workers to learn new skills, increase your business acumen, and make more direct connections between learning strategy and business strategy.

At this level you are paying more attention to key business and performance metrics like quarterly sales figures, current market capitalization of the business, the customer service team's net promoter score (NPS) or year-over-year safety incidents, while also conducting more research on competitors. You minimize the amount of L&D jargon when talking with stakeholders and maximize keywords associated with the business.

Here you also begin taking small steps to have a bigger voice in helping the business diagnose performance issues, launching pilot projects designed to partner with the business on needs assessment, and choosing the appropriate performance solutions.

Level 4: Learning Consultant

At the fourth level of maturity, you begin to act more as a *Learning Consultant*. Here the door opens wider for you to become more like a consultative business partner by applying all the knowledge and experience gained from previous maturity levels.

Needs analysis grows more common and business partners more often grant you additional time upfront to accurately diagnose problems before jumping to solutions. You are invited to the conversation earlier. Business partners get more involved in conversations about business processes and real problems they're facing before simply ordering training.

Some functions at this level begin using design thinking with clients, a framework for creative problem solving that uses a co-engineering approach to help L&D partner with the business to keep the focus on the end user—the learner.

Even at this advanced level, you continue to hone skills necessary for effective consulting, such as asking probing questions, being critical thinkers, saying "no" gently but effectively, and communicating clearly with business partners.

Learning Consultants will continue to experience resistance to their changed roles, but when you do, you will leverage your resources to bring outside voices and data necessary to support the outcome. You understand it can be powerful to connect the business to external, respected industry experts who can share a similar message and reinforce their point of view. Sometimes skeptical business managers simply need to hear a new voice.

Level 5: Trusted Learning Advisor

The fifth and ultimate stage of maturity is the *Trusted Learning Advisor*—what many of us might consider the holy grail.

Trusted Learning Advisors possess the toolkit of skills, knowledge, and experience gained at earlier stages of the maturity model—

including practitioner experience and knowledge of latest learning strategies and of next-generation learning technologies—but also bring advanced power skills including communication, critical thinking, influence, storytelling, empathy, and trust building.

Trusted Learning Advisors are regularly invited by stakeholders—who have experienced their skill and impact as Learning Consultants—to help consult on vexing performance problems before a solution is considered. They are given more time and space than Learning Consultants to apply their earned expertise in both problem identification and solution selection, with the understanding that learning might not be the necessary remedy.

Trusted Learning Advisors have mastered the art of gently and skillfully pushing back and saying "no" without saying no where needed. They are able to identify and craft a message that says, "Here are the reasons why you don't want us to execute your order." They understand business partners are often under pressure to quickly resolve performance issues, but still are able to resist rushing into decision-making around learning solutions.

Trusted Learning Advisors ask the right questions to get the big picture, focusing on both short-term and long-term needs of business partners as well on improving organizational capabilities. They are often deeply ingrained in the business, looking proactively for problems to solve before the business even knows they exist.

Trusted Learning Advisors also make sure their brand, professional reputation, past successes, and relationships all align to communicate their value.

Applying the Maturity Model

This five-stage maturity model can be used to evaluate your own situation and adjust your approach relative to where your organization currently is, directing where you put your focus when it comes to building your practitioner skills, cultivating relationships, and developing your team.

While change starts with you, you'll always be working within the boundaries of where your organization and stakeholder view you today. Every organization is at a different level, and the level of change they're willing to embrace will always be relative to where they see you on the maturity scale.

It's important to evaluate yourself and your team separately—growth may be occurring at different rates. Additionally, it's important to evaluate how your stakeholders and your organization view the L&D function. It's possible to have an L&D function that can or is operating in a Trusted Learning Advisor capacity, but is not supported or recognized by the organizational culture, stakeholders, or executive leadership as such. Although you may consider your practitioner skills in the Trusted Learning Advisor range, it doesn't matter if your stakeholders or organization do not view you in the same manner.

It's important to stop and reflect on yourself and where you sit in the maturity model. You don't label yourself as a Trusted Learning Advisor. But you can and should know whether you have the skills or behaviors of a Trusted Learning Advisor and how others view you. Conducting the analysis of yourself, your L&D organization, your stakeholders, and your organization will help you to develop a picture of how far the evolutionary journey will be for you and your team to Trusted Learning Advisors. As long as you know where you are and what you're working towards, you can develop a path forward.

EXERCISE
Your Turn

Take a moment to reflect and answer the following questions:

- Where do you fall in the model?
- Where does your organization view you?
- Where do your stakeholders view you?
- Where do you view your L&D function?

L&D Practitioner Skills Inventory

While we are shaping change and building a culture of learning, we're simultaneously facing a number of hard-hitting challenges like skills gaps and ballooning attrition rates that challenge our progress. For practitioners, it can feel like there is no room or time to focus on our personal growth.

This is a mistake.

We must be continuously learning and growing alongside our talent. The maturity model is one tool to utilize to gain perspective. The next tool is taking inventory of your L&D practitioner skills to identify your strengths and your areas of developmental opportunity. This type of inventory should be done on a recurring basis (at least once a year) to make sure you are continuing your progression of development and lifelong learning.

The more you know about your craft and the more you respect the work that goes into being an L&D practitioner, the more seamless your evolutionary journey into Trusted Learning Advisor becomes, and the further away you move from being an order taker.

EXERCISE
Your Turn

Flip to Appendix V and check out the Skills Inventory Matrix. Put aside time today to complete your skills inventory.

Celebrate your strengths, and then make a plan to close the gap on the skills that need further development. This is a necessary step in your evolution toward becoming a Trusted Learning Advisor.

Developing Deep L&D Knowledge

Developing the right power skills and personality traits is a big part of achieving practitioner status, but all those skills won't earn you credibility and respect if you don't have a comprehensive foundation of knowledge in L&D.

So, while you are working hard to exercise your power skills muscles, don't overlook staying current on the latest thinking and practice in the essential L&D knowledge-based skills. The following are examples of the L&D knowledge-based skills you should be competent in as a practitioner:

- learning theories
- evidence-based research
- instructional design
- organizational development
- principles of human-centered design
- evaluation and measurement of learning
- principles of adult learning
- training design and delivery
- the role of bias and diversity, equity, and inclusion (DE&I) in learning
- facilitation skills
- new digital tools for learning delivery and management
- change management
- human behavior

An understanding of each one is necessary to help you develop as a well-rounded L&D practitioner. Any one of these could be necessary or called upon in your role as a Trusted Learning Advisor. If you do not have a thorough understanding of each area listed above, this is a great starting point for you to begin focusing on what skills to develop next. At minimum, start with a Google Scholar search for each to begin building more theoretical knowledge.

As a Trusted Learning Advisor your organization will rely on you to be an expert in your field. If you're going to advocate for a certain type of training, you need to be able to present an evidence-based argument for it. And the same applies if you advocate against training as the solution.

Tools and Resources for Theoretical Competence Building

Learning is continual and there will always be more to learn. You will never be fully competent in all areas at the same time; the breadth of what we need to learn is expansive (as demonstrated by the list above). But being all-knowing isn't the attribute that we're trying to project as Trusted Learning Advisors. We want to project a level of unconscious competence in key areas of L&D and conscious competence in emerging business trends or new areas, paired with the self-awareness to recognize our limitations.

The tools can serve as your arsenal of skepticism-busting backup to build others' confidence in you. If you take the time to select the right high-impact resources and stay up to date on industry trends, you'll be able to tailor these tools to fit different situations.

Here are some of the tools you need.

Good Stories

As referenced earlier in the book, developing a collection of personal anecdotes that provide compelling use-case examples helps your stakeholders connect the dots between theoretical and practical real-world application. Stories demonstrate a track record of understanding and competence.

If you don't have any stories of your own, borrow outside stories and tell them from your point of view, giving credit as appropriate.

Case Studies

Like your personal stories, these are examples of practical applications that help make the business argument for or against something. Case studies are incredibly useful for helping your audience see how something might benefit them, by showing how it worked for a similar business or scenario.

Develop your own case studies based on your work. And not just success stories, but also stories of failure. Each failure is still a positive data point for what did not work, and can be just as valuable as, if not more valuable than, the success stories.

If it's too early in your career, there are plenty of industry case studies to leverage. Harvard Business Review (HBR) has online case studies based on real-world scenarios from Harvard Business School, which can be a good place to start looking for examples.

EXERCISE
Your Turn

Reflect for a moment. Are there any initiatives, projects, or programs your team has completed in the last year that can be turned into a case study? Ask your team for their thoughts. Chances are there is a case study waiting to be produced. Aim to find at least one example, and pull the team together to contribute to the activity.

Reliable Research

Make a habit of quoting or referencing reliable research when you speak and keep sources handy to share with colleagues who want to know more. Just one word of caution: there is a lot of junk "science" out there and even more misinformation, especially on social media. The quality of the source is important. Your personal reputation and our industry reputation depend on it.

A reliable information source provides a well-reasoned theory and scientifically backed methods. It comes from a well-established organization and the research has been conducted and reviewed by qualified and competent individuals. Make a habit of always tracing information back to the original source.

Here are some common places to get information, in order of trustworthiness:

- peer-reviewed academic articles (trustworthy)
- trade or professional articles or books (moderately trustworthy)
- consumer magazine articles and reputable media outlets (moderately biased)
- websites, blogs, and other online outlets (often significantly biased)

When talking about reliable research, I'm specifically referencing published research that is peer-reviewed and lays out details including a hypothesis, methods used to collect data, details on how the experiment was designed including control groups, and the results. These studies have been reviewed with repeatable results by qualified peers.

Be sure to take a hard look at the whole picture of the study before you hitch your wagon to that data. Review the bibliographies published with these articles to factcheck the sources for yourself. I recommend starting any of your research with Google Scholar which searches through scholarly literature and academic resources.

Another source of quality, reliable data comes from trade or professional organizations and industry analyst firms. These organizations publish research, blogs, whitepapers, case studies, courses, magazine articles, and many other types of content. Examples of highly regarded sources of data include McKinsey & Company, the World Economic Forum, Deloitte, Gartner, and Forrester.

There are more sources of information out there that can be reliable. But you'll need to do more legwork to verify sources and information if you pull from media-type resources. Media in all its forms, for example, can be biased. While reputable organizations like the *Wall Street Journal* or the *New York Times* are hopefully sharing accurate information, media often has an agenda—sometimes transparent and other times well-camouflaged. Still, well-established brands in magazines and newspapers can be good sources of information if you practice your critical thinking skills and separate the information from the author's point of view.

There also well-developed associations and resources online that are written by knowledgeable and responsible contributors, such as the Association for Talent Development (ATD) and the Society for Human Resource Management (SHRM). But if this content isn't vetted, edited, or reviewed by professional or credentialed experts, assume that all facts are questionable until you've verified them with another reputable source.

There is plenty of published research available in the field of L&D and taking a self-directed and critical thinking approach to building your base knowledge will help you develop a growth mindset that will serve your end goal in more ways than one.

For example, you can read about Jean Piaget's discoveries in cognitive development, Malcolm Knowles's theories on adult learning, or explore how time-honored memory models like Ebbinghaus's Forgetting Curve influence learning. Or pick up books authored by noted experts Will Thalheimer, Nigel Paine, Donald Kirkpatrick, or Jack Phillips. And one book that should be required reading for every L&D practitioner—*Make it Stick: The science of successful learning* by Brown, Roediger, and McDaniel. Check out Appendix III for a list of suggested books.

Lastly, there are dozens of excellent certification and degree programs that can provide a broad slice of theoretical knowledge in L&D. Courses at top-rated universities delve into the inner workings of the human mind and explore cognitive behaviors to understand how adults learn best, such as the University of Pennsylvania's Chief Learning Officer doctoral program. But these types of education programs are only one way to develop L&D practitioner skills. Not everyone's path will look the same. If you are starting at a different point, consider beginning your development by researching the topics listed above.

This type of activity gives you an opportunity for exercising your critical thinking skills and comprehension muscles, while simultaneously building your background theoretical knowledge in L&D. It can also serve as an asset you can consider sharing or publishing.

EXERCISE
Your Turn

Build your theoretical knowledge by researching a knowledge-based skill topic listed above using peer-reviewed journal articles, then write up a literature review on what you've read summarizing the information and establishing your point of view. Consider reviewing five to seven peer-reviewed or academic articles, and include the following:

- Describe the topic you are investigating and why it is important to the field of L&D.
- Provide a "big picture" overview of the literature.
- Identify themes and trends in research questions, methodology, and findings.
- Synthesize what you've learned (provide a re-organization of the information that gives a unique meaning based on your comprehension).
- Review your output with at least one peer.

Experience Reigns Supreme: Gaining Practical L&D Experience

Developing theoretical skills is easier than the practitioner skills. The theory can come from reading and listening, and can be accessible anytime whereas the practical skills comes from... practice—which is more limited and time-bound. Therefore, extra effort has to be put into developing the practical side of L&D practitioner skills. When you are learning or gaining experience, nothing beats doing. You know that's how your learners learn best, when they have the opportunity for hands-on practice and real-life application. The same applies to you as you develop your practitioner skills.

Opportunities to gain experience come in many different forms. It could be collaborating on a high-stakes learning project in your organization with someone more experienced, a stretch assignment where you intentionally seek out a learning opportunity in another area, or a small side project to give you a chance to apply your theoretical knowledge in practice.

Ideas for gaining experience:

- **Conduct fieldwork**: Even in the most constrained circumstances, you can build your practice by doing fieldwork. Create an environment where you're learning by being out in the field with the learners. Go investigate, be bold, empower yourself to do your due diligence. Sometimes it's easier to ask for forgiveness than permission to do the right thing. Uncover their problems. And when solutions are dictated, where possible, create two solutions: what was asked for, and what you believe is the right solution. Test both. Measure both. Use the data. Even if the second solution isn't used, you can add it to your portfolio/use cases for future use.

- **Stretch assignment**: For myself and my L&D team, one of the big areas of development focus has been stretch assignments that provide opportunities to learn and grow. Stretch assignments push you past your comfort zone, but not too far where you burn out. This can include temporarily joining a new team, such as the instructional design team or learning technology team, to shadow and develop new skills. Stretch assignments can be self-created and do not have to only be internal to your organization. Recently I had a new L&D practitioner reach out to me on LinkedIn offering her time for three hours a week for a mentorship stretch assignment. We picked a topic she wanted to develop her skills in, and I gave her small tasks to complete. In a mutually beneficial manner, she gained exposure to a new organization and ways of working with a new leader while working on a small project to build up her portfolio while I invested my time in coaching her.

- **Small prototype/pilot projects**: Prototypes and pilots are low-cost/no-cost opportunities you can create to try out new skills, tools, or technologies and build up experience. They are particularly useful for learning tech work and many offer trial or sandbox environments where you can gain exposure and experience.

- **Industry associations**: Look for opportunities to collaborate with someone from an association such as ATD, Training Industry, or Chief Learning Officer. Industry associations are great places to network and find/create opportunities to collaborate with someone from another organization.

- **Freelance work:** Consider setting up a profile on a gig economy/freelance site such as Upwork or Fiverr to offer your services and give you an opportunity to gain more experience.

- **Volunteer:** Non-profit organizations are a great place to practice your skills while giving back to the community at the same time.

- **Apprenticeships:** One of my favorite ways to gain experience is through apprenticeships programs. Apprenticeship training programs are specifically tailored to ensure you develop the skills employers want, and are typically paid roles compared with internships which are typically unpaid.

Where your experience comes from is unimportant. All experience counts toward the packaged value that you represent to your organization.

Old ways of thinking relied on specializing in one category within the L&D field. Some people spent their entire careers as instructional designers or project managers, never once setting foot in front of a class to teach. Others sat comfortably in management positions overseeing the pieces and parts, but never really engaging with learners directly.

In a way, we perpetuated the silo effect. Not only was L&D operating within a silo inside organizations, but each arm of L&D was operating within its own silo inside the department.

Today we are steadily changing the way we think. We are better together. Agile, cross-functional, collaborative L&D teams deliver greater impact and value.

EXERCISE
Your Turn

Challenge yourself with at least one stretch assignment every six months. Pick from the focus areas above and develop experience in that area until you have theoretical and practical knowledge in each area.

Practitioner's Toolkit

The most important part of being an L&D practitioner is your practitioner's toolkit. A toolkit is comprised of the many resources available to you as an L&D practitioner to support you in your daily quest for problem finding and problem solving. In our field, there is no shortage of support tools available. In fact, there is an overwhelmingly expansive breadth of tools spanning many forms from concepts, methodologies, frameworks, theories, best practices, case studies, and learning technology tools... to name a few. There are too many for us to be experts in each, but it is our responsibility to have an awareness of each and an understanding of when to utilize the necessary tools based on the situation.

As a Trusted Learning Advisor, we need to have an understanding of the learning tools available and strive to have the largest toolkit possible with a clear understanding of the application, the outcome, and when to use each tool. For example, an L&D practitioner should know which learning methodology is applicable, when a use case for VR might exist, or whether an LXP is or is not an appropriate solution. This is our responsibility as practitioners, to know every single tool out there, every use case possible, how it works and how it doesn't work, so when there's a business problem we can go into our toolkit and say, "Okay, for this business problem, this is something that we can use to help support this initiative," —rather than somebody giving us a tool and saying, "Hey, go figure out how you can use it."

It's also important for us to remain agnostic toward providing preferential treatment to a specific tool. As Maslow once said, "If the only tool you have is a hammer, it is tempting to treat everything as if it were a nail." With this approach, we remain single-minded and apply the tool indiscriminately. Part of being a Trusted Learning Advisor is being open-minded and using the appropriate tool depending on the context or situation. Our stakeholders expect that we have a broad range of knowledge and a broad range of tools.

For a comprehensive list of the tools you should have in your practitioner's toolkit in addition to those provided in this chapter, check out Chapter 10.

At this point in the book, you have developed a deeper awareness of the foundational skills you need to be a Trusted Learning Advisor and evolve past order taking. But now I'm going to throw you for a loop. In the next chapter I will share insights into how we get a seat at the table—we take the order. There is, however, a difference between taking the order and being an order taker. Stick with me.

KEY POINTS

- To be a Trusted Learning Advisor requires in-depth knowledge of L&D.
- Both theoretical knowledge and practical experience are needed to develop well-rounded L&D practitioner skills.
- Our field, like our learners, is constantly evolving and we must stay in front of it to keep our skills fresh and relevant and demonstrate our expertise—which requires us to develop deep knowledge.
- Use assessment tools, such as the L&D Maturity Level, or a skills inventory, to measure where you are today and identify what you need to develop for tomorrow.
- Take action to build your skills—conduct research and fieldwork, utilize stretch assignments, create small prototypes/pilots, volunteer, or leverage apprenticeships or mentors to gain practical experience.
- Create a comprehensive practitioner's toolkit to ensure you have a breadth of exposure and experience to the many tools available to support you.

Taking the Order

08

"The important thing is not your process. The important thing is your process for improving your process."

HENRIK KNIBERG

Trusted Learning Advisors Take the Order

Yes. You read that correctly. But hear me out. This dictum may sound counterintuitive to the whole premise of this book. It isn't. Taking the order is, in fact, an indispensable initial strategy on which all the other skills and strategies build as a Trusted Learning Advisor.

Why?

Taking the order sends the message to your stakeholder you are willing to help. It opens the door to the relationship, and it provides the opportunity for you to demonstrate your capabilities as consultative business partners and Learning & Development (L&D) practitioners. Taking the order, however, is not the same as being an order taker.

Taking the order is where the work begins.

You Can Only Help If You Have a Seat at the Table

To be transformative, and to prove your worth to the organization, you first have to be IN the proverbial room. What you do after you get in the room will determine which path you choose (order taker or Trusted Learning Advisor). To stay in the room and have a seat at the table, you say, "Yes, I can help" to your stakeholders—you accept the challenge and immediately proceed to taking the order through the intake process.

Approached with a Trusted Learning Advisor mindset, the difference between *being an order taker* and *taking the order* is glaring. Being an order taker means you are taking the order and executing it as-is in a passive manner without proper intake and analysis. Taking the order as a Trusted Learning Advisor means you are being a consultative strategic business partner by listening to your stakeholder's request and then taking time to conduct your own due diligence discovery process of gaining deeper insight into the problem/situation/challenge.

Think about medical practitioners who are (generally) considered Trusted Advisors. You might visit them with the intention of giving them an order based on your findings from a quick Google search. The medical practitioner will take your order (listen and capture the data) but will conduct their own due diligence (take vital stats, ask additional question, run tests) before drawing their own conclusions.

This is a perfect example of a Trusted Advisor taking the order. Being a Trusted Learning Advisor and taking the order can (and should) coexist.

Taking the Order: The Four-Step Process

When I think about L&D processes, Guy Wallace is the first person that comes to mind. Guy is an author, instructional architect, performance analyst, Trusted Learning Advisor, and career-long advocate for incorporating processes into L&D. He seemed the natural fit for asking what his advice would be to Trusted Learning Advisors on the importance of having a process. He shared the following with me.

> If I could provide one piece of advice to L&D practitioners, it would be to develop a process. The process helps to set expectations with the business, control costs, resources, and ensures the proposed solution solves the problem.
>
> Understanding your own process and methodology and where data comes in affects your ability to do the work as you go forward. But a

lot of people don't have a solid process. Take the order and follow your process.

Managing expectations, creating consistent stakeholder experiences, and defining clear problem statements are three of the many valuable outcomes resulting from following a process for taking the order. The baseline fundamental process I've followed with repeated successful outcomes is IDAD: Intake, Discovery, Analysis, Decision.

Figure 8.1   IDAD

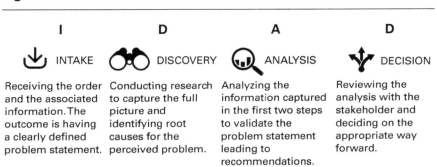

I	D	A	D
⬇ INTAKE	🔭 DISCOVERY	🔍 ANALYSIS	⬈⬋ DECISION
Receiving the order and the associated information. The outcome is having a clearly defined problem statement.	Conducting research to capture the full picture and identifying root causes for the perceived problem.	Analyzing the information captured in the first two steps to validate the problem statement leading to recommendations.	Reviewing the analysis with the stakeholder and deciding on the appropriate way forward.

Intake

One of my least favorite parts about visiting a doctor is their intake process. On my most recent visit, the doctor's office sent me paperwork to fill out online before my visit. As instructed, I took the time to fill it out at home. Once I arrived to the doctor's office and signed the clipboard stating I had arrived, I was handed another clipboard with several pieces of paper—which seemed very familiar to the online set of paperwork I'd already filled out. And yet, I filled it out. Again.

Next, the nurse practitioner escorted me back into an examination room, and guess what she did?

Correct—she asked me the exact same questions I'd already answered on the forms. But this time something was different. Now she was entering the same information on her iPad. As someone who loves process improvements, I was itching to call out the obvious opportunity that existed for both her and every patient to save time.

And finally, once the doctor arrived, what did she do?

Yup!

Repeated the exact same questions. Is this sounding familiar to your experiences?

The problem here, besides the lack of efficiency and annoyance, is that by the time I've answered the same questions multiple times, I grow more impatient, less responsive, and end up providing less information to the doctor, resulting in a poor description of my ailment and possible misdiagnosis on their part.

I mention this example because these same challenges can apply with your stakeholders if you have ineffective or inefficient intake processes. Who your stakeholder communicates with and how the information is captured can have a direct impact on the upfront quality of understanding the problem, and a downstream effect on the output.

The order intake process is one of the most important parts of any stakeholder relationship.

Understanding the Intake Process

A process is a series of steps or actions taken in a set order to achieve a defined result or outcome, providing control and structure. In other words, processes describe how something is done, enabling you to analyze and focus on how it can be improved. After all, "how" something is done determines how successful the outcome will be. As a Trusted Learning Advisor, one of the most important processes you have is the intake process.

The intake process is a planning methodology designed to capture all relevant/required information to articulate and clearly define the problem, and ensure both you and your stakeholder are aligned. Think of the intake process as your playbook on the tasks you and your team will need to perform to understand how to support your stakeholders' orders.

A well-defined intake process can be an important determining factor in your stakeholders perceiving you as an order taker versus Trusted Learning Advisor, as well as determining the likelihood for the outcome of success for the project. The intake process is a critical component of relationship building and has a direct impact on the overall health and performance of your relationship and projects with your stakeholders.

Intake processes:

- **Improve consistency.** A formal intake process helps to improve the quality of the experience your stakeholder has with whoever on the team is their first point of contact. Intake processes enable us to achieve repeatable success through consistency and standardization from one project to the next. When the process is in place and followed, you will know the right questions have been asked and the necessary information has been captured to help you/ your team measure, monitor, and control the project's risks and progression.

- **Gain alignment, prioritization.** Rarely does your L&D function have only one stakeholder or one project happening at any given time. If your intake process practices lack structure, low-priority or low-value projects can enter your pipeline, causing unnecessary strain on your resources. With multiple stakeholders and projects aligning to potentially different priorities, an intake process can help you to prioritize the projects by providing the structure to capture the necessary and consistent information, regardless of who is conducting the intake.

- **Support project portfolio stability.** A healthy portfolio of projects can be maintained by ensuring you have the documented information to minimize scope creep or shifting benchmarks on a project. Often you have projects that span months of development, and what was approved and discussed five months ago may need to shift or look like a different need today. Projects may have insufficient data, vague objectives, minimal sponsor support, or outdated cost estimates. Utilizing the intake process to align with your stakeholder at the outset helps to maintain a portfolio of healthy projects, with the right components to set us and our stakeholders up for success.

Intake Channels

The intake process takes into consideration the channel through which the stakeholder may engage L&D, which may vary. Orders are generally received through three channels:

- via email, to someone directly or to a generic inbox
- via an electronic request form
- verbally

Some organizations allow any/all intake channels, whereas I encourage streamlining those channels where possible.

Of course, you cannot stop and should not deter those side conversations about opportunities with your stakeholders. It would be counterproductive if, following the verbal request, you then redirected your stakeholder to fill out a form. As a Trusted Learning Advisor, your role is to make the engagement experience for your stakeholders smooth and easy where possible. If you've had an initial conversation with the stakeholder, it should immediately be followed up with utilizing a database-type tool, SharePoint for example, to capture the initial information. Doing so would trigger the start of the intake process where you or someone on your team would contact the stakeholder to have a secondary discussion to capture the rest of the information needed to determine the problem statement and move to the Discovery stage.

Capturing all opportunities (orders) into a database is extremely important. Besides ensuring the capture of consistent required data, the database allows for you to provide metrics, such as number of requests, status of requests, etc., to demonstrate the productivity level for L&D. I've worked with several L&D functions that were not telling the story of just how busy they were because they didn't have this data. They could provide the data for the number of projects completed or in progress, but they were not telling the story of how many orders they received, how many went through the IDAD process, how many did not move forward, and why they did not move forward.

After following the IDAD process, a significant number of projects were determined by the team to be outside the scope of a training or learning initiative. By identifying this before project execution, L&D was saving the organization time and money. But by not capturing this level of data and reporting these metrics, their full value proposition was being overlooked—a consistent issue we face in L&D. Make sure to track tasks that have a level of effort, even when the decision has been made to not proceed with the project.

Part of the evolution in having your stakeholders see you as Trusted Learning Advisors includes utilizing tools, such as processes, to standardize and minimize the number of variances in their experiences, particularly during intake, with your team, which builds trust. Trusted Learning Advisors proactively define and set the processes and share them with stakeholders during the initial relationship-building.

Setting Intake Expectations

In my experience, most of the orders I've received have been reactionary and needed "immediately" according to the stakeholder. Designing training solutions is similar to building a house. To build a house you need a plan; you need blueprints. Although I might want my house to be built in two weeks, it takes time and due diligence and I'm reliant on my contractor (Trusted Advisor) to guide me through the process, including providing accurate and realistic timelines.

Proactively communicating your formal process with your stakeholders, embedding the process in your daily activities, and including it in your solutions enables you to separate the individual from the activity. By saying, "this is our process," you are establishing boundaries and signaling that a defined protocol exists and needs to be followed.

My response to the initial stakeholder request usually sounds like this: "Yes, we can help you, but there are a few tasks we need to do beforehand. We have a process to follow to make sure we capture all the necessary information to ensure we're giving you the right solution, using resources effectively, and not missing anything."

How your stakeholders feel when first entering a relationship with you or even returning for repeated opportunities matters. How you manage the intake process is imperative to how well you will be able to deliver on expectations. The intake process helps to set the tone of the relationship and create boundaries and expectations from a tactical and strategic perspective. Intake processes help build trust between you and your stakeholders by giving them a sense of security and safety in your abilities to be a Trusted Learning Advisor. It is one of many signals you can send to your stakeholders indicating you are trusted professionals and practitioners.

Dr. KimArie Yowell, Chief Learning Officer for Rocket Central, shared her insight into the importance of setting expectations with the stakeholder during the intake process:

> When these requests come in and we just take them without setting expectations, without doing our due diligence, it is unclear what impact and value the intervention will have on the business. I often advise my team on the importance of doing the work that matters most to our overall strategic business goals.
>
> Therefore, there will be times we have to have a candid conversation with our business partners about what we're actually trying to accomplish. It may take you longer, but what's harder in the beginning is easier in the end and produces the real value-add.

As Dr. Yowell notes, conversations with the stakeholders might be more challenging in the beginning, but ultimately will lead to more value in the end.

The ability for you to navigate the relationship with your stakeholder and move the needle from being perceived as an order taker to Trusted Learning Advisor starts during the intake of each request. It starts by establishing an intake process for stakeholder requests (orders). The systematic process that you and your team follow for how the order is received and the way in which you respond is paramount for your success.

Be sure you have a clear and documented intake process followed by all.

EXERCISE
Your Turn

Take a moment and reflect on your intake process. Ask yourself: What is my L&D intake process? When I receive an order from my stakeholder, what steps do I take? Are my steps the same steps my colleagues take, creating a consistent approach and experience for stakeholders? Am I sure?

Discovery

In the Discovery phase you are playing the role of researcher or detective. Your stakeholders have given you a few clues during intake, but now you need to discover the rest of the story, the bigger picture.

Uncovering the What, the Why, and the How

Underneath the initial request from your stakeholder lurks the real problem. The problems your stakeholders think they have are usually symptoms of something else. Determining the root cause analysis or unpacking the request to find the real hidden problem is the undercurrent of the Intake and Discovery phase. The three key questions you should be able to answer by the time the Discovery phase is completed are:

- What is the problem we are trying to solve?
- Who is it a problem for?
- And why is it a problem?

Context is everything. It's important in every aspect of L&D, from contextualizing content for learners to understanding the context and situational awareness of the order from your stakeholders. What is driving the request from your stakeholder? Did their boss tell them to put something in place? Did they run an employee survey that instigated the request? Are SLAs or quality metrics not being met? Is it important that people are able to apply the learning solution on the job? Or do they just need performance support-type job aids? Do people need to learn a topic or a behavior, or a task?

Put yourself in the shoes of the stakeholder to understand what they are trying to accomplish and why. For example, let's say you worked in a call center, and you received an order to produce training that helped reduce call time. Before you jump into executing the order, you need to understand the why. There can be many factors that influence call time. Do the agents understand the products? Do they know how to use the technology systems? Do they understand the tools available to support them on the call? Are they skilled in de-escalating situations? The longer call times may be a symptom of a larger issue, but without asking additional questions, the deeper problem will be left untreated. These questions and findings would be uncovered in the Discovery phase.

Asking questions during Intake and Discovery helps you gather the necessary information to understand the context and situation. But if not conducted correctly, it can come across as being combative or challenging. It can be as simple as the tone being used. Maybe the explanation the stakeholder gave wasn't as comprehensive as you needed to understand the full picture the first time. Instead of challenging the stakeholder request, you are challenging your understanding of the problem and the request. You are seeking clarity. For example, you could use the following to ask for additional information: "I think I've missed something. Can you help me understand this better?"

You do not want to come across as immediately challenging; you want to be seen as curious and interested. For example, work with the stakeholder to identify how the learners would practice their proposed solution and what it would look like when applied on the job. Doing so can help the stakeholder think deeper about the request.

The conversation might start like this: "The learners will be expected to apply this learning on the job. To do so, we need to build in practice exercises to make sure learning transfer occurs back on the job. What would that practice look like? How would they actually do this on the job, and how could they practice for it?"

Loren Sanders, CVS Learning Executive and Trusted Learning Advisor, shared with me her approach in the discovery phase to capture the necessary information:

Every request we receive starts with the questions like: "What do you want the learner to be able to do?" and "How is the learner measured on their performance in this role?" One of the key L&D objectives is bridging the gap between these two questions. If you ask the business, "How is this person measured in their current role doing this job?" the business can talk to that. This allows us to reverse engineer and devise our metrics strategy during the analysis phase. This, in turn, brings us closer to the desired outcome.

Following Loren's approach and partnering with your stakeholder on identifying the performance outcomes is a powerful approach to gaining alignment with your stakeholder.

In the Discovery phase, you will encounter stakeholders that may not have the time or energy to think as in-depth as you need them to in order to help you gain the full picture. Some stakeholders want to hand you the order and move on. In those instances, the discovery process can feel isolating.

If the stakeholder doesn't provide with you the necessary information, it's important to figure out who you can talk to in order to answer questions such as:

- Who can I talk to that knows the business?
- Who are the learners I can talk to and understand the problem from their perspective?
- Who are the SMEs (subject matter experts)?
- Who are the high performers?
- What is the level of stake for the business: low, medium, or high?
- What are the potential project constraints?

If the stakeholder can't dedicate the time necessary for your Discovery questions, have them redirect you to the person who can.

Check out a comprehensive list of questions to be asking your stakeholders in Appendix II to complete your due diligence information finding.

Discover the Learners

The Discovery phase is largely focused on uncovering the problem from the perspective of the stakeholders and learners. This provides you with an opportunity to uncover their challenges, and gain insights into aspects of the problem the stakeholders might not be aware of.

Both qualitative (e.g. one-on-one interviews, focus groups, observations) and quantitative (e.g. surveys) research may be used during the discovery phase. Qualitative and quantitative data gathering follows a specific science. There is a significant artform to crafting the approach and questions to capture the correct, necessary, and unbiased data. Trusted Learning Advisors Guy Wallace, Patti Shank, and Will Thalheimer have all published extensive material on capturing learner data. If you are familiar with design thinking, Discovery would be the empathy phase. And if you are not familiar with design thinking or qualitative/quantitative data gathering, add this to your upskilling to-do list.

Ultimately the Discovery phase is where you are learning more about the identified challenge from those who are impacted (the learners). You might already be thinking this, so I will say it for you—access to learners is not always possible. I've been in multiple situations where constraints exist keeping us from the learners. Sometimes an unsigned contract may be a factor. Other times it has been the result of corporate politics/organizational hierarchy. On occasion the stakeholder simply didn't trust us enough (yet) to talk with learners individually without a manager present (rarely will you get the insight needed if the manager is present).

In these situations, you need to be creative and use tools like learner personas (fictional profiles that represent the target audience including characteristics such as backgrounds, demographics, skill levels, platform usage, etc.). Another approach is connecting with colleagues who have knowledge of the business or of the learners, and understand from their perspective.

If your stakeholder pushes back against you having access to learners while you are still building trust with them, be respectful of their position. But be creative, even if that means you and your team are roleplaying what it might be like to be in their shoes.

Analysis

In the Analysis phase, the examination and evaluation of the collected data occurs, giving the necessary context to make the data useful and to tell a story. This is where the intelligence gathered goes from just being loosely related pieces of data to a finished product that is useful for the following decision-making phase.

When you say "yes" to an order, you are taking on responsibility to conduct proper analysis, including an outcome indicating whether L&D is the solution to the problem. You follow the data to a conclusion. You do not manipulate the data to fit a preferred conclusion. If your research concludes that success is outside the realms of L&D, you communicate that finding, along with your reasoning—for the benefit of the company.

Guy Wallace provided the following advice to me:

> Don't be somebody who takes an order and executes it without generating data that can be used to assess if you are on the right track or if you are doing the right thing. I don't think people should be blindly taking orders. But I do think they should take the order and insist on doing an analysis.
>
> If the stakeholder resists doing analysis, then you've got to make a decision. Is this the hill to go to battle on? Or should I just salute, go off and do it, telling them it might not solve their problem, but I'll go do it for you?

If your data analysis indicates the approach is the wrong approach to take, it is your responsibility to document the finding and ensure the client recognizes what the data says. It doesn't mean it will change their mind, especially if the order is coming from someone else but being delivered through them, but at least have it documented and have them physically sign off on it. At the end of the day, it is a business decision, not an L&D decision. As a Trusted Learning Advisor, you can leverage the data and your expertise to advise other options but, in the end, you may need to build it the way they requested anyway.

Analysis Tools

Once you have gathered your data, part of analyzing the information is to synthesize it and identify synergies and themes. A number of tools are available to support you in the analysis phase depending on the depth of analysis the initiative needs.

For example, you could analyze the interviews with learners in a formalized process known as a thematic analysis, which involves coding the data, creating themes based on the interview data, and generating definitions of themes. This is an approach that helps you capture and utilize the voice-of-the-customer (VOC) which, in this case, is the learners.

I love quantitative and qualitative data. Particularly when it comes to L&D, I love the qualitative data, especially the voice of the learners. It's no longer our voice, our message, our words but the words of others. Gathering qualitative data, empathy research, and VOC/ voice-of-the-learner (all similar concepts with different language) can be more powerful than our voice. Instead of you droning on from a perceived biased viewpoint, it's the frontline workers voices, colleague's voices, those that are struggling—it's their voices being leveraged. In my experience, stakeholders will argue with my voice, but I've yet to experience a time when they argue with the consolidated voices of the learners.

Data is your secret weapon. And the importance of using data to define your approach and process cannot be stressed enough. Keep in mind the importance of also understanding which data is important to your stakeholders. Sometimes data you think is important may not register on the same level for others. Ask for and document the metrics that are meaningful and valuable to your stakeholders. It doesn't mean you don't capture the data you think is meaningful. You continue to capture your data, but just ensure you are also capturing the data relevant to your stakeholders.

There are qualitative and quantitative software analysis tools, such as Dedoose and Nvivo, that can be leveraged, but unless you have a significant amount of time to invest in learning the tools, along with a high-profile project with a substantial budget for the analysis phase, I would not recommend these tools. I have only used these tools in academic research. You can use Microsoft Excel for basic coding and thematic analysis.

Six Sigma methodologies, fishbone analysis, process map analysis, or empathy mapping from design thinking may also be beneficial framework-type tools to leverage. But again, these would not be part of your normal routine. To give you an indicator of how often these might be used, I would estimate I use them 20 per cent of the time.

If it's a smaller order (not a global/corporate initiative, smaller audience, low-cost), I utilize general Microsoft products for any analysis, documentation, and presentations.

Lastly, in the Analysis phase, you define a (possible) revised problem statement based on the broader research and a detailed definition of the learner's needs and an outline of the proposed recommendations. The output of your Analysis phase can include:

- a summary of findings, including thematic analyses and revised problem statement(s)
- a recommendation of approach
- estimated costs
- risks

Decision

After completing the due diligence with Intake and Discovery, followed by the Analysis of data, you move into the Decision phase where you and your stakeholder decide what action to take regarding the initial order, based on the intelligence gathered along the way.

Guy Wallace shared with me the four outcome options he proposes in the Decision phase:

> I use data to inform all my projects. When it comes to the Decision phase, I'll give the client four options: 1). End the project because it doesn't make any business sense; 2.) Defer the project because there's something else that needs to happen before we continue; 3). Modify the project because what we've learned through Discovery and Analysis suggests we need to change how we go forward; 4.) Approve the project and begin.

Guy beautifully articulates the four potential outcomes in the decision phase—each decision outcome with their own nuances. I would add one additional option: to pilot/prototype an alternative solution to increase the dataset.

The Decision phase takes significant preparation. Although characteristics of a Trusted Learning Advisor have been shown to your stakeholder through the structured framework followed during Intake, Discovery, and Analysis, the Decision phase is your real opportunity to demonstrate the breadth of your skills and will require many of the characteristics identified in previous pages. Specifically your influencing, negotiation, consulting, and communication skills will be brought to task in the Decision phase.

Why?

Most likely what you have uncovered during the prior phases is going to lead you in a different direction to what your stakeholder originally proposed. I find it prudent as a Trusted Learning Advisor to go into the Decision phase as if the stakeholder is going to stand firm on their original position, and I need to influence them to see an alternative path—based on data, of course.

Your approach during the Decision phase is to lead with data and to approach the discussion and decision in a level-headed and non-emotional way.

The following are four best practices to follow to help you prepare for the Decision phase:

1 Have clear documentation on the synthesis from Intake, Discovery, and Analysis.

2 Include all potential outcomes and their associated consequences or risks.

3 Include VOC quotes from learners, where relevant.

4 Research similar problems and bring forth case studies and external data to support your position.

The outcome of the Decision phase is to generate potential courses of action/next steps with your stakeholder. As with the other phases, document the discussion and decision with your stakeholder for future reference. You never know when your stakeholder may need a reminder of the decision.

Although stakeholders can often be resistant to following processes like IDAD, the processes are in place to safeguard the stakeholder's order and the investment in the order execution.

The following is an example of when following the IDAD process would have saved the stakeholder, L&D function, and trainees time and money.

A manager in a gas and utility company came to L&D complaining that his plant was experiencing an unacceptable level of errors in jobs that required employees to work from a blueprint. The manager was adamant in demanding a new training course be developed to help his people read blueprints, a demand that led to all employees in a maintenance area being trained. This required time away from the job, overtime to allow other employees to attend the training, and high course development and delivery costs. And due to the urgent nature, the manager provided no time for upfront due diligence from L&D.

L&D complied with the order, and yet after the training was delivered, the same levels of errors and rework around blueprints continued.

In a second attempt to solve the problem, the L&D group followed their due diligence process and used a front-end analysis to determine the root cause of the problem. Sure enough, the problem wasn't due to inadequate skills or knowledge—employees already knew how to read blueprints. The problem instead turned out to be environmental. The blueprints were stored in a small room without an adequate indexing and filing system. Employees couldn't always locate the prints they needed. In addition, the room's lighting was inadequate, so employees often missed key details on the prints.

The solution? An updated indexing and filing system with improved room lighting.

As a Trusted Learning Advisor, you support your stakeholders and keep your "seat at the table" by taking the order and following a structured process to guide you directionally. Following the IDAD process, or any framework, is not a guarantee you will be able to change the position of your stakeholders, but it is a guarantee you will take the steps to provide the intelligence necessary to make a sound and structured business case for the appropriate path forward that serves the stakeholders and the learners.

When you take the order, ask yourself, am I adding value with this order? If you aren't, figure out how you can. Sometimes just executing the order is the value-add. It might go against your beliefs as a practitioner and cause pain on the inside, but it can build goodwill and provide continued opportunities in the future.

Resistance from your stakeholders is part of the process and part of your reality—even after providing a well-structured argument supporting your position backed with data. The next chapter will provide insights for managing and overcoming resistance from stakeholders.

NOTES ON IDAD

There is no shortage of models, processes, and acronyms in our industry. For the most part, models, processes, and acronyms help with framing and remembering. Whether you agree with it or not, most of us can cite out the ADDIE model acronym. I struggle with throwing one more into the mix. However, as Trusted Learning Advisors, part of our job is to have a large toolkit filled with different acronyms, frameworks, methodologies, and technologies, and to know when to use (or not use) each one. Much like with building a house—you wouldn't use just one tool—the same applies to L&D.

When it comes to models, methods, etc. there are two disclaimers important to recognize as Trusted Learning Advisors:

1 Methodologies, processes, and frameworks are not intended to be applicable in every situation. As discussed earlier, what worked there may not necessarily work here. There is no "one-size-fits-all" model to follow—the context of your situation is going to help determine the approach you should take to be successful within your organization. The idea is to have an awareness of as many methodologies and processes as possible and to understand when to apply them in the right situations.

2 Frameworks, processes, methodologies, in my opinion, are guideposts. They are intended to be agile and are ripe for continuous improvement. IDAD is no different. The intention with this model for taking the order is to provide a guidepost for key steps to include when you are taking the order to ensure the stakeholders' and L&D's best interest are being represented and ultimately keeping you "at the table."

KEY POINTS

- Trusted Learning Advisors always take the order—which might sound counterintuitive, but it's an important step to ensure you are in the room to have the necessary conversations and drive transformational change.

- Without an intake process, you risk being order takers who take on projects with unsupported information or data, projects where training cannot solve the problem, projects where you are set up to fail before you even begin.

- The process for taking the order is a critical component of relationship building that helps stakeholders see you as a Trusted Learning Advisor while also having a direct impact on the overall health and performance of your relationship and projects with your stakeholders.

- Think of the intake process as your playbook on the tasks you and your team will need to perform to understand how to support your stakeholders' orders.

- Process for taking the order—IDAD: Intake, Discovery, Analysis, Decision:

  o Intake: Receiving the order and associated information. The outcome is a clearly defined problem statement.

  o Discovery: Conducting research to capture the full picture and identifying root causes for the perceived problem.

  o Analysis: Analyzing and synthesizing the information captured through Intake and Discovery to validate the problem statement, leading to a recommendation on how to proceed.

  o Decision: Reviewing with the stakeholder and deciding on the appropriate way forward to solve the problem.

Overcoming Resistance: Yours and Theirs

09

"Resistance is the first step to change"

LOUISE HAY

You've read this book. You've applied the principles. You've put in the work to begin your transformation into a Trusted Learning Advisor. And yet on your first, second, and third engagement, you feel your stakeholder is being resistant to your ideas and keeping you at arm's length. It's probable even after you've followed the IDAD process from Chapter 8 to gather the data to demonstrate to your stakeholder why a better solution exists, and you still hear the word "no."

Frustrating? Yes.

Alarming? No.

There will be resistance from stakeholders as you are building trust, forming relationships, and establishing your credibility. Getting those who've been conditioned to see you in certain ways to accept the authenticity of the "new you" can be a tall order. Many stakeholders have long viewed Learning & Development (L&D) as passive order takers—and we often justify their beliefs by willingly acting in subservient ways.

As a result of those hardened views, there will be many situations where you'll meet resistance as you are working to reposition yourself as a Trusted Learning Advisor. The reality is, when you first begin acting in more of an advisory fashion, some stakeholders may view you as challenging their decision-making authority or their conclusions about the "best ways" to address the learning needs of their employees.

In other cases, you'll find stakeholders resistant to your requests for needs analysis or additional investigation into performance problems because they don't want to be bothered to think as in-depth as you need to successfully plan and execute the project. Some stakeholders simply want to hand you the order and move on.

Don't forget, you are attempting to reverse a century-old mindset that the business knows best, and you are an order taker. Unfortunately, your stakeholders are not going to immediately greet you with open arms. Change isn't easy and ultimately, you are now pushing back against the old behaviors, albeit ever so slightly, to redirect and reestablish your relationships and ways of working. It will take time. And you will hear the word "no". The power isn't in the word "no." The power is in how you overcome their resistance.

When the Stakeholder Says No

"No" can be an uncomfortable and threatening word. It starts for many of us at a young age when our free will is challenged by adults telling us no when we want to do something; it takes away our control. The visceral reaction to the word "no" is developed early and continues through adulthood. "No" creates a barrier; it feels resistant. People generally do not like to hear the word "no"—not us, and not our stakeholders.

Although we try to avoid using the word "no" with a stakeholder, we are sometimes on the receiving end of it when we propose approaches or solutions. I've been on the receiving end of "no" more times than I can count with stakeholders early in my career.

When faced with a "no," the fundamental step to take is to listen to your stakeholder, have a dialogue, and understand their perspective.

Of course, just having a dialogue may not change their resistance. Therefore, the following are three strategies to consider when working towards overcoming your stakeholder's resistance:

1 Recognize "no" might mean "not right now."

2 Bring in other perspectives.

3 Start smaller.

No for Now

When your stakeholder says "no" to you, it does not always mean no in perpetuity. Sometimes no just means "not right now." An order taker will take the "no" and be done. A Trusted Learning Advisor will seek to explore and understand the context behind the response and consider what could be done differently to achieve the intended outcome, or the "yes."

It's your job to decipher what the "no" actually means.

In Action

Sujan was an independent L&D consultant working on developing a relationship with Robert, a new potential client. Robert was a learning leader working in a small finance organization and was trying to convince his leadership to invest money to develop an organizational learning strategy—the first investment of its kind at this organization. Sujan's strength was in developing learning organization strategies and he felt he could provide great value to Robert.

Sujan went through the proposal process and was picked as one of the two final vendors Robert's company would be reviewing. Ultimately, Robert's company went with Sujan's competitor. Although disappointed, Sujan thanked Robert for the opportunity and reaffirmed he and his team were ready to work with Robert if and when needed.

Several months later, Sujan reached out to Robert to see how the initiative was progressing. The intention behind the call was not to sell anything but rather a true welfare check on the project. Sujan wanted Robert to be successful with or without his help.

Robert shared that the project had stalled, and nothing had progressed in the few months. It turned out that after Robert's company picked the competitor, Robert's boss never signed off on the cost for the project. Curious, Sujan asked him why the signoff was not approved.

"Money. She doesn't want to invest the money."

Sujan pressed him further, "But why?"

There was silence. Robert didn't know. He hadn't asked one of the single most important follow-up questions we should always be asking for clarity... why?

As a favor, Sujan spent time with Robert to help him recraft the pitch and coach him to present it back to his boss. This time, however, Sujan gave Robert an important piece of advice to help him gain deeper insight into the "no".

"If she says no again, follow up with this question for clarity: If you are not comfortable signing off on this proposal, what will need to change in order to make you feel comfortable to move forward?"

Feeling prepared, Robert met with his boss, received the "no" again but followed Sujan's advice. By asking the probing question, Robert uncovered that unbeknownst to him, a similar initiative had been executed several years before he joined and was unsuccessful and costly. His boss did not want to follow the same approach again but was, however, open to finding a new approach for developing their learning culture.

Part of overcoming resistance is asking the questions about what doesn't work, why, and how you can recalibrate it so it will work.

Often "no" is the first step in a dance that takes you into reframing orders into solutions. Understanding the reasons behind a "no" requires not only active listening and understanding, but for you to pay more attention to the emotions that are shaping your stakeholder's choices and actions.

REMEMBER

The following is a great question to ask when you receive a "no" to help you gain further perspective into their reasoning and how to overcome their resistance: "If you are not comfortable with [this], what would need to change to make you feel comfortable to move forward?"

Bring In Other Perspectives

Think back to the last time you received uncomfortable news from a Trusted Advisor. Maybe it was a doctor sharing an unwelcome diagnosis, a dentist prescribing a root canal, or a mechanic recommending you replace one of the most expensive parts of your engine. Although you trust them, you might not trust them enough to simply take their diagnosis/recommendation without further validation. It might make you feel more secure to get a second opinion from someone else to provide you with additional data points and confirmation.

As informed consumers, we often seek second opinions—this is us doing our due diligence. Your stakeholders are no different! Particularly as you are in the early stages of demonstrating your evolution and building trust and credibility, your stakeholders might value a second opinion. It's possible your stakeholder simply isn't ready to listen, trust, or recognize you as a Trusted Learning Advisor yet. That's okay, they are being informed customers. Until we have reached Trusted Learning Advisor status, and possibly even after, our voice and perspective may not be sufficient.

One approach I've often used to help stakeholders overcome resistance is to rely less on my voice and more on the voice of others such as other L&D practitioners, third-party data, voice of the learners, and leaders from other organizations. After all, as Trusted Learning Advisors, we are conduits and connectors. We have, or should have, relationships throughout the organization and the L&D community. Therefore, when our voice is not enough, bring in outside voices and perspectives.

For example, I will bring in another stakeholder from within the organization who faced a similar challenge and facilitate a conversation between parties. This is an example of when tapping into our L&D champions throughout the organization can be an asset in helping your stakeholder recognize a broader picture or solution. It is also another example of why building relationships both in and outside the organization is such a critical component of success for Trusted Learning Advisors. I've also introduced into the conversation external L&D practitioners and stakeholders in a similar position from other organizations.

Start Smaller

Sometimes our goals may be too aspirational, which causes our stakeholders to say "no." Rather than trying to convince your stakeholder for approval on an entire project, consider a smaller initiative, such as prototyping/piloting, to gather additional data to strengthen your case.

Prototyping is a low-cost or no-cost approach to create a minimum viable product (MVP) which gives your stakeholders something to react to. Following a "try and learn" approach creates space for incremental understanding and awareness, easing our stakeholders into a new position.

Decisions are not always binary; they land somewhere on a spectrum. Our goal with our stakeholders is creating an on-ramp for shifting perspectives along that spectrum. Think of it not as trying to change their mind, but rather opening their mind to see things from another perspective. Often, it's as simple as taking a step back together and seeing how the learner would benefit and the impact it would have on the organization, and then moving forward together with an aligned understanding.

When the stakeholder "no" occurs, and it will, it is important to not immediately react. Take a breath. Pause. Apply the three strategies just discussed:

1 Recognize "no" might mean "not right now."

2 Bring in other perspectives.

3 Start smaller.

Don't take the "no" personally, and suspend your inner child from having a visceral reaction to being told "no." Don't further directly push your agenda. Listen. Really listen to your stakeholder, acknowledge their viewpoint, and try to understand their position.

Once these steps have been taken, then you can determine if you want to challenge your stakeholder.

To Challenge or Not To Challenge: That Is The Question

When a stakeholder approaches you with an order, they are inadvertently asking for your help (albeit maybe not in the language or manner you might prefer). When someone asks for help, you help them—the situation is no different with the orders from our stake-holders. The question is whether we challenge their perception of the problem or their solution (the order).

Understanding when and how to challenge our stakeholders is a true test of a Trusted Learning Advisor, as it requires a high level of sensitivity and situational awareness.

There are several perspectives to consider when you are determining whether to challenge your stakeholder:

1 The status of your relationship.

2 Whether your stakeholder wants you to play the role of Trusted Learning Advisor or order taker.

3 The role of the stakeholder in project success.

4 Whether the order is merely a check-the-box request.

Establish the Status of Your Relationship With Your Stakeholder

Early in the relationship-building process, for you to build the trust, you often start as an order taker to get that first order, establish your credibility, and continue to build from there. Once you have credibility and trust, your stakeholders are more willing to listen to you and to be challenged. But immediately challenging the stakeholder at the beginning of the relationship can result in a strain on the relationship, or in the stakeholder working around you.

Early in my career I recall challenging a stakeholder on their order before our relationship was firmly established. We did not have a communication cadence, had not built trust, and I was not acting as a consultative business partner. It resulted in my stakeholder bypassing me and setting up a direct partnership with a third-party outside vendor to complete their request. At the time, I didn't even know using third-party vendors was a possible outcome or risk of me not executing the order.

Although bypassing L&D was against the process, the stakeholder had a deadline to meet and took measures into their own hands to ensure completion. Had I recognized we were in the stage of forming our relationship, I would have spent more time conducting my due diligence to understand their needs. In doing so, I would have learned the request was a timebound requirement that needed to be executed as-is, and not the right opportunity to flex my challenging muscles. It was a good lesson learned for me, and one I haven't forgotten.

Another example of the importance of determining the relationship status before challenging stakeholders occurred when I came into my first Head of Learning role. I had ambitious goals of developing a best-in-class, innovative learning organization, filled with engaging programs that would win awards.

After a few initial conversations with stakeholders, I recognized my team and I had a lot of work to do on the functional side, as my predecessors had not established relationships or built trust with our stakeholders. Although I had grandiose plans, the reality was that that wasn't what the business wanted or needed yet. They didn't care whether we won awards. They didn't care if the solutions were innovative. They wanted effective and efficient content produced as quickly as possible to minimize the pain of the learners and improve performance challenges.

I immediately had to recalibrate my vision to the needs of the stakeholders, and realize that the order that the business wanted me to take was just to put pen to paper and get it done. They didn't care what it looked like aesthetically; they just needed the training to work. And I needed to produce something in the first 90 days to demonstrate support.

The final product was a very ugly performance support tool—a PowerPoint manual. It was not pretty, and it went against everything I believed in; it was just hardcore standardization of what they needed to know. The output was not something the team wanted to create or something I would put in my portfolio, but... it worked. It won us the graces of the stakeholders because we established credibility with the business that we could deliver what the business needed.

From there, I was able to use the credibility established as a springboard to build the Learning Institute, advocate for larger investments of money for L&D, and ultimately make an impact on the business. But it all started with a realization that I had to recalibrate my approach. Rather than taking the estimated six months to deliver the solution I wanted to build, it needed to be an immediate response to the stakeholder order. I needed to show them that I heard them and that I filled the order. As a result, it bought me that credibility. It allowed me to start pushing into the more transformational side of learning. But I had to wait to get the credibility; it had to be earned.

This illustration is a testament to the need for (and skill involved in) looking at the situation as it is and evaluating where you are in your relationship with the stakeholder, rather than what you would like it to be. Projecting too far into the future or coming in as a disruptor at an inappropriate time can undermine your ability to effect meaningful change later.

While acting as an order taker initially can open the doors, build the trust, and even meet the immediate needs of your clients, the real art is learning when to transition to a Trusted Learning Advisor role. Staying too long in the order taker role will only reinforce a traditional subservient function from which you are trying to break free.

To avoid being perceived as just an operational function, after two to three successful "wins" in your new relationship you should begin to shift toward a more consultative identity. This will invariably involve increasing the frequency and the intensity of challenging new orders. The courage to step up will serve to build your credibility as a strategic thought partner and a reliable coach to the business and its leaders.

Choosing the right timing in challenging stakeholders is crucial, and it requires patience, humility, flexibility, practice, and wisdom.

EXERCISE
Your Turn

Reflect on your career for a moment. Can you recall a time when you challenged your stakeholder too early in the relationship? What would you do differently this time with your newfound knowledge of being a Trusted Learning Advisor?

Order Taker or Trusted Learning Advisor—What Do They Want?

Much of the time stakeholders just want something to get done and executed, but it doesn't mean they just want an order taker. I've worked in multiple organizations where the feedback from the stakeholders was that L&D was just an order taker, not innovative, and not a business partner to them. "L&D is just doing what they are told. Where is the value-add in that?"

The irony in those comments, which I'm sure you have experienced, is that L&D would say, "We've tried to bring them ideas and stop taking orders, but the business wasn't interested." There is often a tension in the relationship between L&D and stakeholders: "Be our business partner, but don't push back when we tell you what to do."

One of the reasons for this tension is that if you wait to be a business partner or to be innovative, by the time the order comes in, it's already too late. If the business is submitting an order, most likely they are reacting to something and, in their minds, it just needs to get done. Your opportunity to establish yourself and your relationship needs to start long before the order comes in. Therefore, it's important to analyze the situation to determine what is needed at that moment—an order taker or a Trusted Learning Advisor?

An initial order may require rapid action to fix an acute, time-sensitive problem through training. Sometimes being a Trusted Learning Advisor means playing the role of order taker temporarily to get through the immediate crisis, with our eye on future stability where we'll have the opportunity to have greater influence.

When someone shouts "Fire! Fire!" you do not have a debate on whether the fire exists, or what the root cause of the fire is, or whether you should use water buckets or a hose to extinguish the fire—everyone works together to minimize damage and put out the fire as quickly as possible. Afterwards you can evaluate what happened, identify the root cause, and try to put protocols in place to ensure another fire doesn't happen. Maybe you even share with others what happened so they too can minimize their future risks.

As a Trusted Learning Advisor, we need to be aware of when a reactive "fire" is happening, versus an opportunity to provide our consultative learning expertise.

Initial orders are also (in)direct tests of your boundaries, and are a delicate balancing act. The start of the relationship is the appropriate moment to discern your stakeholder's underlying needs and intent. The nuance that makes all the difference in how you proceed is figuring out what the requestor truly wants. Do they just want you to take the order and make the problem go away, or is the person looking for a thought partner and an active problem-solving participant?

Sometimes the business wants an order taker—no more, no less. "I just expect L&D to be a transactional function, not a partner or a consultant." The business may want a certain number of units produced in a certain amount of time with a certain level of quality. Many business leaders include L&D in the realm of order takers: I need you to do this thing to achieve a specific outcome. There's a mindset that they, the business, will submit a request to L&D to accomplish certain tasks in a certain way.

In Practice

Lauren was recently promoted to the role of L&D manager. One of the first requests she received was to develop 10 eLearning modules. The L&D team had not established themselves as Trusted Learning Advisors and Lauren was still building up her relationship and credibility with her stakeholders. In the early conversations, Lauren shared with her stakeholders the philosophy of their work: we're creative, we like to do things very graphically, we aim to create phenomenal learning experiences in our work. The stakeholder seemed interested in their philosophy, at least responding with "Yeah, great! We want all of that." Lauren, excited her stakeholders seemed to be aligned with their vision, set off with her team to complete the request.

It wasn't long before Lauren realized her first lesson learned. After spending time developing several prototypes, Lauren showed them to her stakeholder. She shared their development process for the remaining activity, in alignment with the initial vision proposed, to which the stakeholder reacted in disagreement—"Oh no, we don't want any of that. We want it to look exactly like everything we already do."

Confused, Lauren recalled the prior alignment conversation with the stakeholder. "Yes, that all sounds great but we really just want this to be done asap like the last batch of content created. We can just do it ourselves if it's going to be a problem. It will only take us four hours to do it with the templates we have." This sent a signal to Lauren that the stakeholders wanted them to take the order and execute it as-is, and if they didn't, the relationship would risk being damaged.

Feeling deflated, the team proceeded to build the modules to match the existing design, just as the stakeholder had requested. However, thinking as a Trusted Learning Advisor, while Lauren's team completed the order per the request, Lauren took time to develop a prototype of what the content could look like by following their originally proposed vision of incorporating Learner Experience (LX) design elements.

During the next review meeting with the stakeholders, Lauren walked through the order as requested. Although with a tepid response, the client seemed pleased with the content meeting. Lauren then said, "We wanted to show you another potential version we call 'the art of the possible' for what future content could look like." Lauren proceeded to show the stakeholder the version she envisioned for what constitutes "good" learning content.

Silence.

The stakeholder sat up in their chair and exclaimed, "Yes, this is it. This is exactly what we want! But why don't they all look like this?"

Lauren explained they followed the requirements given, but rather than belaboring the reason, she took it as an opportunity to ask for several additional weeks to revise the other modules into the prototype format, to which the stakeholder agreed.

In the end, the stakeholder wanted Lauren to take their order and complete it as-is based on the lack of trust, credibility, and time. Lauren took the opportunity to complete the order without challenging the client while creating an opportunity to demonstrate "the art of the possible" in a manner that did not threaten the client or use the word "no." Doing so evolved the stakeholder's expectation from order taker to Trusted Learning Advisor. And, magically, additional time was made available.

Although it can be challenging to accept that your stakeholders view you and your service as purely transactional rather than collaborative, it's important to recognize and acknowledge their position in order to overcome their resistance.

Navigating the role of Trusted Learning Advisor is more akin to a game of poker than solitaire; it's dynamic and fast changing. You don't know what cards the other players have, the extent of their experience, emotional maturity, business philosophy, etc. Each environment for being a Trusted Learning Advisor is situational and unique, so each approach needs to be uniquely tailored.

Stakeholders Play a Role in Project Success

Some of the resistance you may feel from the stakeholder can be the "just get it done" mentality. It's highly probable the stakeholder is pressed for time and wants to pass off the order. It's also possible no one has helped the stakeholder understand the complexities of successful learning or change initiatives, including the fact that training is not always the single solution, even though most would prefer it was.

Part of your role as a Trusted Learning Advisor is helping your stakeholders see there are other factors that play into solving a problem that sit outside of just a training solution—and often involve other parts of the organization, including the stakeholder. The training product is one component. Change management, stakeholder engagement, and leadership support are all necessary ingredients for ensuring successful training initiatives—and often outside your control.

Let's say your stakeholder requests that you create a 75-minute virtual training program that will create a coaching culture. You can develop a training program on the knowledge and skills needed to build a coaching culture. However, the program creation and deployment alone will not guarantee success. There are many variables that come into play that you need to help your stakeholder explore by raising awareness on the risks and asking the associated questions. Do people recognize or understand that a coaching culture doesn't currently exist, but a need for one does exist? Do they care? Do they believe creating one is important? Is the stakeholder aware that a 75-minute virtual course will not create a coaching culture?

Culture training and the associated change management takes time, significant time. Does the stakeholder recognize it is a culture shift which means leadership at all levels will need to buy in and support it? Is there a plan for how the environment will support this culture change?

By helping our stakeholders think through these deeper questions, you are helping to set expectations that the training initiative itself is not the sole remedy and cannot be a standalone solution. Ultimately you are helping to protect the stakeholder, but also your team. If you take the order and execute it as-is and it fails because no outside support was given, no one blames the stakeholder. They blame you, when, in reality, you have very little control over what happens outside of the classroom and back on the job.

It's your responsibility to help your stakeholders recognize that L&D can't be the only ones accountable for the success or failure of the programs. Your stakeholders also play a key role in the success of learning initiatives—it's just often not presented to the stakeholder in a manner where they recognize or acknowledge they have any accountability. The most successful initiatives I've seen executed with the broadest impact are those where the stakeholder is an active participant and champion for its success.

It is your job as a Trusted Learning Advisor to help the stakeholder understand they play a critical role in the success of learning initiatives.

Checking the Box

Some of the orders you receive in L&D equate to a check-the-box exercise, meaning the training is taking place because it needs to fulfil some sort of requirement (often compliance), and is not necessarily meant to improve work performance or change behaviors. Compliance and regulatory training tends to be check-the-box-type training, as demonstrated by the following practitioner story shared with me.

Several years ago, Yuan worked for a large financial institution that was under investigation for money laundering activities. After an investigation into the institution, it was determined that a number of employees had enabled activities that fell within the classification of money laundering. The company had not invested enough time to ensure all employees understood the concepts of money laundering;

therefore, the company was required to change the behaviors of the entire company within a short timeframe.

Instead of thinking about this as a cultural issue or change management issue in the organization, it became a training issue, and the order was given: every single person in the organization needed to take anti-money-laundering training within four months.

This project, or order, had the highest visibility within the organization. When Yuan asked about the measurement of success, he was told, "Every single person must complete the training. We need a 98 per cent completion rate."

Yuan and his team tried to incorporate the science of learning and design the training so they could measure learning transfer to help people change their behavior—but at every turn they were shot down. Defeated, he knew this was nothing more than a check-the-box exercise, to be able to say, "Yes, every person took anti-money laundering training." But did the learners' behavior change? Did they learn anything? Who knows! No one was measuring it.

In the end, the initiative was considered successful by leadership standards—they had a 99 per cent completion rate within the time allotted, and his team was celebrated. But in his eyes, he'd failed. His criteria of success, as should be yours, is whether anyone could apply what they'd learned. Did it transfer back to the workplace and have an impact?

Yuan shared:

> I don't think anyone learned about money laundering, and we didn't change the culture or behaviors. We all knew this was simply a check-the-box program.
>
> These types of epiphanies are hard when you are a Trusted Learning Advisor. It hurts my soul when I'm forced to work on a project that isn't about learning or improving performance. In this case, it should have been about changing behaviors and helping people, particularly frontline workers, gain the skills they needed to minimize money laundering in their bank branches. But it wasn't.

It is not always clear if an order is only a check-the-box activity. As a Trusted Learning Advisor, we should be as bold as to directly ask, "Is this a check-the-box initiative where we just need to get it done?" It can be a provocative question to spur a valuable conversation—if you have crafted your Trusted Learning Advisor skillset and understand the tactful way to ask the question.

(Hint: this should not be one of the first few questions you ask your stakeholder. You can often answer this question indirectly by the lack of information and interest the stakeholder may have in the project, and then confirm by asking outright.)

EXERCISE
Your Turn

Think back to orders you've received over the years. Do any of them register as check-the-box activities? Would it have been more helpful for you (and possibly time saving) if you knew upfront that they were check-the-box activities? What will you do next time you think the order is just checking a box?

Regardless of how much you try to influence your stakeholders to see their approach may not be in their best interest, you cannot always change their view. In my research with other Trusted Learning Advisors, some suggested that if your stakeholders still want to proceed with the "wrong" approach even after you have shown evidence to the contrary, you should walk away.

I disagree.

A Trusted Learning Advisor doesn't walk away.

A Trusted Learning Advisor discusses, encourages, promotes, and even argues for ideas and solutions that are in the best interest of the stakeholder and the learners. I've never been in a position where I told a stakeholder "no" and refused to proceed with the work. In the situations where I believe a more appropriate approach/solution exists based on data, I will document the data, findings, proposed solution, and potential costs associated with not following the proposed solution, and ask the stakeholder to sign off on it in the Decision phase.

Consider, for example, the resource and cost implications of executing the wrong solution. There is a quantifiable dollar amount that can be calculated for:

- L&D:
  - Time spent developing materials.
  - Additional cost of materials.
  - Time delivering program.
- Stakeholders:
  - Time spent reviewing materials.
- Learners:
  - Time spent in training.
- SMEs:
  - Time spent providing input for developing/reviewing materials.

I encourage you to be bold enough to document the potential costs associated with a potential wrong solution. If your stakeholder wants to proceed regardless of your warning, have them sign off on acknowledging the associated risks and costs. It should not be an act of aggression on your part, but rather a collaborative discussion about you doing your due diligence to capture associated costs and risks. This is expected of Trusted Learning Advisors.

It does not need to be formalized with a printed document and wet signature; it can be as simple as detailing the costs, the discussion, and the decision made via email and asking for a responding confirmation. This is an important step—trust me. I've been in a number of situations where I did not have any form of confirmation of the conversation and their acceptance of the risks, only for the business to accuse me eight months later, after the program failed, of not clearly communicating this risk to them.

Getting documented confirmation provides you with some form of protection against claims of negligence or unprofessionalism if the project does not perform as hoped. It is your role to advise. It is the client's choice to either act on that advice or not. Either way, we would be prudent to document our recommendations, even if only for CYA (cover your a...) purposes.

On occasion, this approach has successfully encouraged the stakeholder to overcome their resistance and proceed with our approach, not wanting to take accountability for the costs associated with being wrong. Or it has given them the courage to take the risks to their leader for their sign-off. But on occasion, stakeholders do still "accept" the risk and we proceed forward... knowing the solution will not solve the problem and we will be back at the table for discussion again in a few months. It's simply part of the process—we will not overcome resistance every single time.

Resistance, both yours and theirs, comes with the territory. Succeeding as a Trusted Learning Advisor requires dealing effectively with the inevitable resistance and skepticism from stakeholders conditioned to see you only as an order taker. Coping with pushback is a natural and necessary part of your evolution and development.

You are here to serve your stakeholders, which means you need to stand up for them and sometimes need to help them see other perspectives. Although "no" may be commonly used by your stakeholders, it's your responsibility to stand the ground and challenge them in a respectful manner—if it serves the greater good.

If the order proposed is not the right solution, you can help the stakeholder by identifying alternative solutions. Invest the time needed before challenging your stakeholder, and if an alternative solution may exist, invest time with your stakeholder to ensure they understand why you are advising against what they have asked. Use the data. Doing so will help your stakeholders navigate through resistance to ultimately land at the outcome that best serves the needs of the organization.

Congratulations, you are almost there! The final chapter synthesizes key points and strategies found throughout the book and distills them into eight best practices of Trusted Learning Advisors. Chapter 10 serves as a great ongoing reference guide for you on your evolutionary journey.

The following strategies can help you overcome stakeholder resistance:

- Offer alternative suggestions: "We can explore this solution; however, I'm not sure it will work for this specific problem. Have you considered 'this' instead?"

- Play devil's advocate: "What happens if we don't do this? What are the outcomes from that?"

- Brainstorm solutions together, involve the stakeholder in identifying alternative solutions.

- Document the associated risks and outcome/confirmation of the decision to proceed. Create a cost-benefit analysis for the risk of their proposed solution.

- Find evidence or examples to support your reasoning or counter their prescription. Doing so will help deflect the response that this is "only your opinion," and help establish credibility in your reasoning.

- Practice roleplaying difficult discussions.

- Have empathy in all aspects of responding to the request.

KEY POINTS

- When faced with stakeholder resistance, remember the following:
  o Don't take the "no" personally.
  o Don't further directly push your agenda.
  o Listen—really listen.
  o Acknowledge their viewpoint and try to understand their perspective.
  o Seek to understand why they disagree with you.

Best Practices of a Trusted Learning Advisor

10

"Strive for progress, not perfection."

DAVID PERLMUTTER

All the chapters leading up to this point have offered you the processes, tools, and structure necessary to support your transformation into a Trusted Learning Advisor. The ingredients are all here, the rest is all about you—your execution, your approach, and your commitment to putting in the effort for yourself, your learners, and your stakeholders. You're taking what you've learned and turning your attention inwards to focus on adopting and refining the best practices that will set you up for success as a Trusted Learning Advisor.

To wrap up this book and synthesize several of the key points, the following are best practices I have leveraged to create and nurture my own career on my journey to being recognized as a Trusted Learning Advisor. These strategies will help you get started toward achieving the same goal. Practice and master these approaches and you'll soon find yourself fulfilling your potential as an evolved true Learning & Development (L&D) practitioner—a Trusted Learning Advisor.

Develop a Trusted Learning Advisor Mindset

The intellectual capabilities of the human mind are expansive. We still don't know what the brain is fully capable of, despite years of scientific studies. One of the ideas behind adopting a growth mindset is that anything is achievable if we set our mind to it—including changing our own mindsets.

We have a certain mindset developed—some are open to change and others more resistant. What we believe about ourselves, and the potential of human talent, is shaped by our role models as we grow and learn. Children learn from parents, peers, and teachers. Adults learn from colleagues, mentors, leaders, and other influential voices in their industries. Our mindset is not predetermined by our genetics; it is influenced by those around us. If you change those influences, you can change your mindset. And since our mindset shapes whether we believe we can do something, it's a powerful force in determining our future success.

You've taken the time to read through this book. Possibly many of the ideas discussed here are abstract, foreign, and maybe feel out of reach. The first step in your journey to becoming a Trusted Learning Advisor is to simply *believe* that you can be a Trusted Learning Advisor. And you can. We all can. You have the basis and foundational information at your fingertips right here. Although your stakeholders ultimately give you the label "Trusted Learning Advisor," it's your behaviors, your expertise, and your own beliefs that lead you to this ultimate path.

It starts with something as simple as seeing yourself as a consultative business partner—a Trusted Learning Advisor. As you begin to see yourself in a different light, so will others. Your mindset is nothing more than a set of attitudes that you hold about yourself or your abilities.

Here are three ways to begin changing your mindset toward recognizing yourself as a Trusted Learning Advisor:

1 Accept a need for change.

2 Identify outside perspectives.

3 Consistently focus on developing new habits.

Accept a Need for Change

In Chapter 2, I discussed the history of our industry and many of the reasons we've been held back from fulfilling our full and true potential. The business case for our need to change can be described in two words: "order takers." For too long we've been treated as order takers, and it is time to change the narrative and perception others have, as well as our own behavior. Every L&D practitioner I've met has agreed that there is a need for us to change, both as an industry and as individual practitioners. We are each accountable.

This book is one of many ingredients to support you through this change.

Identify Outside Perspectives

You do not have to go through this journey/change/evolution alone. In fact, you should not and cannot go through it alone. We—all of us—are in this together and need to support one another in our evolution toward becoming Trusted Learning Advisors.

Build your network. Make connections. Question others. I've yet to meet an L&D practitioner who was not willing to help another learn, grow, and evolve along the way. Be open to feedback but, more importantly, ask for it.

Consistently Focus on Developing New Habits

Although not directly referred to as "habits," this book is filled with best practices, suggestions, and strategies that should become your habits that you can (and should) apply to create success for you, your stakeholders, and your learners.

Consistency is woven throughout the Five Pillars of Trust (credibility, reliability, professional intimacy, intention, and communication) outlined in Chapter 5. Being consistent helps build momentum and self-discipline. Consistency creates accountability which translates to progress and helps you achieve your goals.

Being a Trusted Learning Advisor is not a destination—you don't "arrive," congratulate yourself, and then move on. Being a Trusted Learning Advisor is a continuous evolutionary journey which requires dedication, discipline, and a long-term commitment. Being consistent in your dedication will support you as you build up the necessary habits to continue your evolutionary journey.

When it comes to being a Trusted Learning Advisor your mindset is critically important. What you believe is possible will become possible for you. That means if you're afraid you can't create value for your stakeholders, that fear will become a self-fulfilling prophecy. You can create value. L&D does create value.

Get your mindset right and you have the first key towards building a future as a Trusted Learning Advisor.

Someone once told me, "What follows 'I am...' will follow you." I am... a Trusted Learning Advisor. Say it. Believe it. Now go and be it.

Shape Your Personal Brand

The power of branding is phenomenal. Branding can create loyalty, credibility, consistency, and value—all aspects that you want as Trusted Learning Advisors. More importantly, the true power of branding is its ability to influence your stakeholders to recognize you as consultative business partners rather than order takers.

Using the basics of marketing, a brand—whether it's applied to a product, service, or, in this case, to an individual—is a cohesive identity that makes it easy for others to recognize the value, expertise, competencies, quality, or other attributes that belong to that product, service, or individual. You need to establish your identity (brand) as a Trusted Learning Advisor.

A six-step process can help you shape your personal brand:

1 Identify what you are trying to create.

2 Know your value.

3 Prepare an elevator pitch.

4 Master the art of networking.

5 Create a digital presence.

6 Amplify your brand messaging.

1. Identify What You Are Trying to Create

In your case, you are establishing yourself and your identity (brand) as a credible, respected, trustworthy, consultative L&D business partner (aka Trusted Learning Advisor). All roads in personal growth lead back to the same starting point—self-discovery. Get to know yourself first and decide what your "it" thing is that you want to be known for as a Trusted Learning Advisor. For example, if you're the "it" person for problem solving and you're always there to provide great advice on demand, lean into that and build your brand around solving performance problems.

If your strength lies in connecting the dots and seeing the bigger picture, build your brand around being a *strategic* Trusted Learning Advisor. If you're a natural-born influencer, build your brand around *influencing change* as a Trusted Learning Advisor.

Keep in mind that this is your personal brand and not a replica of some other successful person's approach to being a Trusted Learning Advisor. While you need to highlight relevant skills, pick one that suits you and run with it. I call this my "superpower." For me, my superpower is problem solving and learning. I do not know everything. In fact, I do not know a lot of things. But I know how to learn what I don't know, and I am great at solving problems.

2. Know Your Value

Once you know what direction you're going, build yourself up. Take time to understand the value that you bring to the table. There are specific reasons why you are good at a particular skill and there are likely many examples that highlight your past successes.

What are your differentiating factors from others? Why you? Why and how are you a Trusted Learning Advisor? What value does that provide to your learners, stakeholders, or organization? While this might take time for you to identify for yourself, it's incredibly important to know your value proposition and be able to articulate it to others.

3. Prepare an Elevator Pitch

Be able to clearly explain what you do and why you do it in under 60 seconds, and in a manner that someone can remember—or even better, be able to repeat. This pitch should convey the reason you do what you do. Not everyone has found their passion (yet), their "why" (motivation) behind why they do what they do. If you haven't yet found your passion behind why you are in L&D, spend time doing so. Ask others why they've joined the illustrious field of L&D. Their insights might help you form your own.

I started in the L&D field as a trainer solely for the purpose of getting a job—no altruistic motives. I've since learned over the years the true power and impact we can have as learning practitioners. When we can thrive—we change lives. Learning is the path to unlocking our true human potential. My pitch is as short and succinct as this— *my passion is to empower, enable, and encourage talent to take control over their future through the power of learning.* This is my "tag line," describing my passion for why I do what I do.

What's yours?

4. Master the Art of Networking

Networking is about creating long-term opportunities, not short-term gains. Networks are established through relationships. Relationships are critical to your success as a Trusted Learning Advisor, and important enough that Chapter 6 was dedicated to developing relationships with stakeholders.

But your relationships and networking don't stop with your stakeholders. Network inside the L&D community. Network inside your organizations with learners, finance, IT, frontline workers, and managers. Network in competitive markets and in markets that have nothing to do with your current organizational work. The wider you cast your networking "net," the more you will you gain different ideas and perspectives and ultimately increase your value to any organization.

5. Create a Digital Presence

When you want to learn about someone, what is the first thing you do? Either you ask someone else in your network (hence the importance of networking and relationship building) and/or you Google them. Although I work for organizations, I have a website (www.

keithkeating.com), so when anyone looks me up I have complete control over the narrative I want them to see and what I want them to know about me, my mission, my vision, and my expertise.

My website is my calling card, my brand, my digital portfolio, and my online presence. It gives people an opportunity to learn about me, in my own words, before they meet me. It has also led to a number of new relationships, including mentorships, speaking engagements, and teaching opportunities. Just like any organization or product, without a website, you're basically non-existent.

If you are in your first few years in the L&D field, figure out "who" you are first, build up some experience, and then create your digital portfolio. At minimum, however, you should have a LinkedIn account and be active, at least within the L&D community. Although I am not advocating for social media as a concept, LinkedIn is one of the best platforms/methods to use to build a professional network, to learn as a practitioner, and to share your thoughts, ideas, and experiences with other practitioners. Additionally, it helps cultivate your digital presence.

6. Amplify Your Brand Messaging

Marketing is a powerful tool when used properly, and no one else is going to market you as well as you can market yourself.

Consider writing articles for industry publications and sharing your practitioner views on podcasts or webinars. Offer to speak at local chamber of commerce events or through professional organizations like your local chapters of ATD or SHRM. Share your experience with others.

You are going to need to hustle and be your own marketing agent regardless of where you are in your career. I spend a little time each day working on my brand, whether it be engaging on LinkedIn, researching topics, or connecting with other practitioners. I write proposals for articles and submit them to industry journals (and receive plenty of rejections). I submit proposals for speaking engagements and teaching opportunities and volunteering initiatives (also with a healthy dose of rejection). Mostly, each activity is working towards achieving the next goal I've set out for myself.

It takes work to refine and amplify my branding message. But I love it. I love the challenge, the hustle, and each opportunity I achieve is one that I created. Each level-up or reward point I capture is only meaningful to me.

Your brand is critical, and it takes work. Being successful with your branding and marketing allows people to see you for who you are and what you are—a Trusted Learning Advisor.

Build a Well-Rounded Practitioner's Toolkit

If you are building a house, a hammer will be an important and necessary tool, but it is only one of many important and necessary tools. As a Trusted Learning Advisor, your responsibility is to have a large toolkit filled with many tools. You will most likely not be an expert in every tool in your practitioner toolkit—that's okay. More important is simply understanding them and knowing when and how to apply them. You can always reeducate yourself when the time comes to use them.

Familiarize yourself with every L&D technology platform and every L&D tech vendor. Understand the measurement and evaluation approaches (Kirkpatrick, Philips, Thalheimer, etc.) and understand the differences. Be aware of the five learning theory concepts. Consume the concepts behind problem-solving methodologies such as PDCA (Plan, Do, Check, Act), design thinking, and Agile.

Having generalized knowledge about all aspects of learning theories, tools, frameworks, case studies and methodologies helps you be a credible practitioner.

Your practitioner's toolkit benefits you in your role as a Trusted Learning Advisor by enabling you to back up your claims in conversations with sourced data and as inspiration when tackling a new project. It makes you credible and authentic—necessary components for building trust with your stakeholders.

Let's look at some examples to get you started.

Learning Science, Methodologies, and Theories

An important part of providing expert advice is tying your recommendations to the science-backed principles of learning, design, neuroscience, and human behavior. Throughout these pages I've provided a variety of models and skills that will serve you well as a Trusted Learning Advisor. All of these should be in your toolkit.

Here are some specific examples of additional aspects of the science of learning to include in your toolkit:

- neuroscience of learning, experiential learning, and working memory
- Piaget's stages of cognitive development
- diagram and literature on Ebbinghaus's Learning and Forgetting Curve
- the science behind learner-centered design
- data on the relationship between emotional intelligence and learning
- concepts on the science of durable learning

The following are additional examples of learning theories and methods to include in your toolkit:

- ATD's Talent Capability Model
- 21st-century learning theories such as:
  - andragogy and heutagogy
  - transformative learning
  - self-directed learning
  - experiential learning
  - project-based learning
- 19th/20th-century learning theories such as:
  - behaviorism
  - cognitive
  - constructivism

o humanism

o connectivism

Remember—our stakeholders are not L&D practitioners and don't understand the complex and scientific nature of learning. They aren't commonly familiar with concepts like learning transfer and the need for interleaved practice, elaboration, reflection, and recall. As Loren Sanders, CVS Learning Executive, noted, most stakeholders believe telling equals training:

> I think most stakeholders still subscribe to the idea that if you tell learners something or give them the information, they are going to be able to perform it. They still haven't caught on that telling isn't learning. There's a huge expectation from the stakeholder that when you finish training, you are proficient at the job. And there is a learning curve they aren't taking into consideration. Most people come out of training, and they're still learning. They're still figuring out how to make it work.

You are the practitioner, which means you need to gently coach your stakeholders where you can on the science of learning.

Problem-Solving Methodologies

The underpinning of what you do is solving problems. Therefore, it is a critical component of your toolkit to understand various problem-solving methodologies and tools. Like all other tools, there is no shortage of options. Fishbone diagrams, affinity diagrams, benchmarking, brainstorming, Pareto charts, and scatter plot diagrams are just some of the many tools available to you. Personally, there are a few key problem-solving processes I've found incredibly helpful to understand and find myself utilizing on a recurring basis.

The following are problem-solving processes and methodologies I highly encourage you to have in your toolkit:

* Agile
* human-centered design:
  o design thinking
  o Learner Experience (LX) design
  o User Experience (UX) design

- continuous improvement processes:
  - ○ Lean and Six Sigma

Case Studies

Case studies are valuable education tools to help you learn about problems and the detailed approach utilized for solving them. Case studies offer an opportunity to learn from the experiences of others while providing data that can influence the practice of theories. Being familiar with case studies covering the same issues your organization may be facing helps give you insight on possible directions to head toward or avoid.

If you don't have any in your arsenal already, find several high-quality case studies that are relevant to your organization. These case studies are powerful tools of persuasion and are proof that your recommendations can work by using data rather than only your word.

Examples of real-world case studies to include in your toolkit:

- A story about shifting the workplace to a culture of learning.
- A story about learning in the flow of work and its impact on engagement and productivity.
- Case studies on the practical use of learning technologies to enhance learning or improve performance.
- A case study on capability building to create Agile teams to support cross-skilling recommendations.

It's not only important for you to have an arsenal of case studies in your toolkit (most likely you'll end up searching for new ones when each problem/opportunity arises); it's equally—if not more— important to write your own case studies on the problems you and your team have solved. Your practical experience is just as important for others to learn about as it is for you to review theirs. Having published case studies for your own work lends additional credibility for you as a Trusted Learning Advisor.

Choose well-sourced literature or case studies from reputable research firms such as McKinsey Global Institute, Deloitte, Harvard Business Review (HBR), or the World Economic Forum (or all four) to bolster credibility. When searching for any other research, case studies, or data, I recommend you start with Google Scholar instead of Google, to help reduce the number of opinion-based results versus academic.

Learning Technology

L&D practitioners have more technologies and tools than ever before at their disposal to build and disseminate engaging content—and the digital age continues to add more options by the day. It's important to collect data on the viability of different learning technologies for your toolkit.

Examples of learning technologies to include:

- asynchronous learning platform comparisons
- personalized learning plans and assessment
- a list of interactive learning tools for virtual platforms
- use-case examples of learning technologies in action
- artificial intelligence applications in L&D
- articles on emerging ed-tech trends for L&D
- learning experience platforms
- Massive Open Online Courses (MOOCs)
- learning management systems
- learning record systems
- test engines

Your practitioner toolkit can be your most valuable resource. It's helpful to begin building it with organization-specific data. Whatever metrics you've been tracking, collect the historical data on those key performance indicators and build your own benchmarking report. This will steer your toolkit in the direction of being highly relevant.

It can feel overwhelming to look at this list (and I'm sorry to shock you further, but the above is only a partial list; we need to be aware of even more topics like diversity, equity, and inclusion (DE&I) and designing for accessibility), but you're not expected to know everything on day one or even in the first couple of years. It takes time to build up your experience and awareness of the tools.

One of the most important pieces of advice I can share for your practitioner's toolkit is to remain neutral and unbiased. You might dislike Kirkpatrick's five levels of evaluation and love learning management systems, and possibly for valid reasons, but your role as Trusted Learning Advisors is to remain impartial and unbiased, searching for the right tool to solve the problem. The important skillset for you is to think critically about the problem (or opportunity), consider the tools in your toolkit, and then decide on the best approach.

Lastly, having a broad range of knowledge of the available tools doesn't mean you are limited or required to use it as-is. I view frameworks and methodologies as starting points, like structural support, often pulling from multiple approaches to create an approach necessary for the situation at hand.

Subscribing to only one model is limiting. Instead, Trusted Learning Advisors have a broad toolkit, looking to apply the right solution for the problem. There is no one-size-fits-all solution for L&D. The context of the situation needs to be considered. What worked in one organization will not automatically work in another. Be iterative, agile, and creative all while serving your intended purpose.

Treat Technology As A Solution, Not *the* Solution

This is an important statement to make—technology is not always the answer. Technology is an enabler; it is not the standalone solution. Over the last 10 years, our industry has grown victim to the shiny, appealing, alluring draw for technology as the solution. Technology is *a* solution or *part of* the solution, but it is not *the* solution.

Far too many times over the years I have seen L&D practitioners buying into the notion that an LMS, LXP, MOOC, virtual reality, etc. is going to solve their problem, without ever clarifying the problem they are trying to solve or how the technology will solve it, and completely missing the questions, "Will our learners embrace the technology?" and "Does our culture support the use of this technology?" I've lost count of the number of times learning technology launches have failed for the simple fact that the organizational culture did not embrace it, or that the learners were being forced to use the technology outside their flow of work.

L&D practitioners need to take a step back and focus on the basics, such as incorporating more learning sciences and the psychology and neuroscience of learning, and less on the shiny distracting technologies offering the promise of lessening the difficulty or time it takes to learn. We seem to be gravitationally pulled to the bright and shiny objects—often pressured by stakeholders who want learning to be accomplished faster and cheaper. Learning is not easy, learning is challenging. There are steps you can take to lessen the cognitive load and help your learners learn, but this idea exists that there's some sort of technology that will make it easier and faster for learners to learn.

Learning takes time. Until new knowledge can be downloaded directly into the brain, the simple fact that learning is hard and time-consuming does not change... no matter how learning tech advocates try to spin it.

Recognize What Worked Here Won't Necessarily Work There

As practitioner skills and experience are developed, it's important to recognize that each organization, each stakeholder, each business unit, and each problem you face is individually nuanced based on its context and situational analysis. There is no one-size-fits-all with solutions and approaches to problems.

I've worked in many organizations throughout my career, and each one has a unique approach and culture. What worked at one organization isn't going to necessarily work at another. It's not a lift and shift mentality; *if it worked here, it will work there*. It's about context and relevancy. Take the time to learn the context for your stakeholders. Solutions may be different, even if they come from the same source of inspiration. But ultimately, everything operates in context.

As you are building your skills and solving problems, you need to understand the abstract principles behind why something worked in one situation and its context, and then recontextualize it for your organization. I often have organizations say to me, "We want you to do here what you did at X organization." My response is always, "What we did at X worked there. That was right for them and for their culture. Your culture is going to be different. Your leadership is going to be different. We need to first identify the context of your situation and environment."

L&D strategies and tactical implementations are not an exact rinse and repeat model. Their contextual factors are different. It is possible external factors have totally undermined or influenced the success. Therefore, you cannot lift and shift a model or a way of working. Components from Company A could be applicable at Company B, but it takes time to understand the culture and the business before making any determination on what works or doesn't work.

Stay Connected to Your Learners

Above all else, your position as a Trusted Learning Advisor is cemented in your ability to provide effective solutions that create value for your stakeholders. You're not being judged solely on your ability to contribute to conversations; you're judged on the value that you bring to the table, value that is measured in terms of impact.

What organizations need most right now is to maximize their human talent. Specifically, they need ways to keep employees motivated, fulfilled, and productive so they not only achieve business goals, but feel little desire to look for greener pastures. Opportunities to learn and grow are continually cited as a top reason why employees stay loyal to a company. Organizations that don't understand that achieving financial goals is only possible by first focusing on meeting human needs are often those that experience the highest voluntary turnover and the most disengaged employees.

Stay connected with your learners. Capturing the voice of your learners is a powerful way to ensure your learning initiatives are aligned with employees' most pressing or relevant needs, not just what leaders assume those needs to be. Qualitative research, focus groups, one-on-one discussions, observations, and surveys are great tools to capture learner data. As explored in earlier chapters, it's one thing when you present an idea as your own to a stakeholder—it could easily be arguable. But when you capture the voice of employees through qualitative data, it becomes harder for stakeholders to argue against their own people. That makes data your secret weapon.

The more time you spend sitting in the seat of the learner, the better tuned-in you will be to the humans on the other side of the solutions you're proposing to your stakeholders.

Keep Your Expertise Sharp

Expertise takes more than smarts. A good foundation of academic knowledge, theories, and principles is only one component of your expertise as a Trusted Learning Advisor. That knowledge can easily fade if it's not regularly exercised or updated in the context of new research or studies. While college degrees and advanced study in learning theory or cognitive science are helpful in developing your expertise, you need continued exposure to these principles to keep your expertise sharp.

To be recognized as a Trusted Learning Advisor, you need expertise gained from real, hands-on experience. You need a collection of personal stories that demonstrate your expertise by highlighting successes and pivotal moments in your career. It's important to keep adding to your resume, portfolio, and practitioner toolkit.

Continuous improvement and lifelong learning are not only necessary for the evolution of your organizations and your learners, they're necessary for the evolution of yourself.

Endpoints are not compatible with lifelong learning; if you embrace one, you cannot have the other. A Trusted Learning Advisor needs to be fully committed to lifelong learning.

Here are some practical steps you can take to focus on continuous improvement and learning at the Trusted Learning Advisor level:

- Join a community of practice—if you can't find one, start one!
- Monitor industry trends and new insights by attending relevant conferences and reading respected industry publications.
- Make a habit of reviewing new academic research quarterly.
- Give back to your profession by hosting webinars or writing case studies.
- Apply for industry recognition through award programs.
- Exercise critical thinking and establish your own point of view on relevant topics by writing articles to share your experience and thought leadership.

Practice, Practice, Practice

Across the industry, a challenge exists that practitioners, particularly early in their career, struggle with the skillset or experience level to be consultative. Although practical experience is invaluable, there are other ways to build skills. Practice makes you better at something. Therefore, creating the opportunity to practice a skill repeatedly will only make you better at the execution of the skill.

> Practice = Experience + Rehearsing + Roleplay

Before any important meeting, not just those with stakeholders, I practice or rehearse. For some meetings I outline my talking points; for others I script out the entire scenario, thinking through and responding to different potential outcomes. What might they say? What is the question I don't want them to ask—are there any areas of vulnerability I need to consider? And how would I respond to it? Doing this helps me feel prepared while building my comfort level and confidence.

Besides rehearsing, one of my favorite ways to feel prepared is to roleplay scenarios. Roleplaying is a great way to get comfortable with different scenarios before they occur, especially if you are newer in your career. But no matter my years of experience, roleplaying will always be a tool I leverage for myself and my team to help build the skill of practice and preparation.

The following are five roleplay scenarios you can consider using for yourself or your team:

1 A stakeholder submits an order without giving the information behind the request. How do you respond to gather more information?

2 A stakeholder submits an order with a prescribed solution that you do not believe will solve the perceived issue. How do you respond without using the word "no"?

3 A stakeholder does not want to listen to your feedback. What are ways you can help them hear your perspective without being combative or aggressive?

4 How might you convince your stakeholder additional time is needed to conduct discovery and needs analysis for a project?

5 Your stakeholder consistently engages you in a reactive/firefighting manner. How might you approach your stakeholder to help them see the value in bringing you into the discussion before the order has been placed?

In addition to these, consider common themes or situations you have experienced and turn those into roleplay scenarios.

Next Steps: Build Your Own Road Map

There is theory and then there is application. I've spent a good portion of this book talking about the theory behind transforming into a Trusted Learning Advisor. But as you approach "graduation day" (the completion of this book) and begin to move to new levels in your L&D career, application will take center stage as you put theoretical models into practice and apply lessons learned from your experiences in the trenches of the workplace.

As you create your road map, consider these as actionable next steps:

- Invest in self-discovery, beginning with a comprehensive skills inventory so that you have a good idea of where you are now and where you need to go.

- Execute on all activities and suggestions laid out in the previous chapters.

- Begin building your own "table." Instead of waiting for an invitation to the long-sought "seat at the table" with other corporate departments, proactively start the right conversations and create opportunities yourself, inviting business partners and other stakeholders to your table. Start by forming a skills advisory council to discuss critical workplace learning needs and industry trends. Bring in outside resources, and host events to showcase ideas.

- Create a Partner Expectation & Commitment Charter. This provides the framework for sitting down with your stakeholder to engage in your relationship discovery, asking the right questions and defining the scope of services, deliverables and expectations.

- Create a standardized intake process. As discussed in Chapter 8, your intake process should include an established methodology for conducting needs analysis as well as standard questions you'll ask stakeholders when they approach you with a request.

- The following are examples of questions to ask your stakeholder. These should help you capture the full picture and uncover more of the real story:
  o What's driving the request?
  o What problem is being solved?
  o How was the problem identified?
  o How are employees measured on performance in their roles?
  o What are the possible project constraints?
  o How might managers support training when learners are back on the job?

Measure your progress against the road map as a routine part of your growth process. Take time to reflect on your recent activities and realign your plan for becoming a Trusted Learning Advisor after every significant interaction. Formalize the process by implementing a post-implementation review process (PIR) and use the results—good, bad, or indifferent—to create your own case studies for your practitioner toolkit.

The journey towards becoming a Trusted Learning Advisor takes a long-term commitment. Progress will be slow at times. You will encounter moments when you feel uncomfortable, experiences when you feel underinformed, and times when you question your dedication or ability. These feelings are a natural part of the growth process.

Learning isn't easy, and no matter how much our stakeholders wish we could speed up the process of learning, it takes time—even for us, L&D practitioners. The rewards of the journey will be many, for you, your business partners, your organization, your learners, and for the standing of the L&D profession. We are all standing together at a fork in the road, facing the choice to embrace this change and transform into Trusted Learning Advisors or get left behind as our traditional order taking roles grow increasingly irrelevant. The choice is yours to make.

KEY POINTS

- Develop a Trusted Learning Advisor mindset.
- Shape your personal brand.
- Build a well-rounded practitioner's toolkit.
- Treat technology as A solution, not THE solution.
- Recognize what worked here won't necessarily work there.
- Stay connected to your learners.
- Keep your expertise sharp.
- Practice, practice, practice.

Conclusion

"If you continue to do what you've always done, you'll continue to get what you've always gotten."

HENRY FORD

Measuring the Distance Between Order Taker and Trusted Learning Advisor

Imagine all the qualities of a Trusted Learning Advisor on one end of a spectrum and all the qualities of an order taker on the other. Each of us falls somewhere on that spectrum. Understandably, most of us have a lot of progress to make to move that needle closer to the Trusted Learning Advisor side. It's a continuous journey, not a destination.

Take time right now to think about yourself and how your L&D department interacts with your organization. When you take on a new project or attend a meeting, what happens? What is the intake process like? How people approach you and how you respond indicates the status of your current role and what opportunities exist for developing your skills as a Trusted Learning Advisor.

Order takers are content to accept information without questioning it and are eager to please by delivering what is asked. Trusted Learning Advisors look for long-term satisfaction over the instant gratification of "good job." They challenge assumptions and aren't afraid to go against the status quo or ruffle a few feathers. They ask "why?", knowing that it may lead to difficult conversations—or more work or no work at all. Trusted Learning Advisors uncover the "need," not just the "ask," because they are focused on getting to the root cause and solving the problem.

When you start to work on a request, what's the first thing you do? Order takers get busy mapping out the scope, budget, and deliverables. Trusted Learning Advisors go straight to the big picture, making sure that they can articulate the business problem and impact.

Order takers work in a transactional and tactical manner, while Trusted Learning Advisors are strategic and relational.

Trusted Learning Advisors show up to be a resource. When they speak, the focus is always on business needs. If they make a recommendation, it's calculated and often includes solutions beyond their own products and services.

And finally, how does work come to you? Order takers tend to be reactive, always responding to needs. In most cases, they wait for other departments to voice a need or directly request training interventions.

Trusted Learning Advisors take a proactive approach. They've become experts at anticipating needs and finding opportunities to get involved before their help is solicited.

Without self-reflection, a well-defined roadmap, and finely tuned GPS, you're likely to spend time wandering the back roads rather than taking a direct route toward building the kind of skillsets needed to become a respected, sought-after Trusted Learning Advisor in your organization.

Where are you in the journey?

_____

What are your roadblocks to moving ahead?

_____

_____

_____

What new skills, attributes and knowledge should you learn to progress?

_____

_____

_____

What Happens If Nothing Changes?

You could put this book down and go back to the way that things have always been—no one would be any wiser. You could continue to spend your time serving your stakeholders as an order taker, creating training with minimal, if any, impact. You could remain safely tucked away in your silo where you don't have to be challenged by or challenge your stakeholders.

But if you do that, you are perpetuating the problem that you already know exists.

You don't have to change, but your stakeholders will. Your stakeholders will find a way to get what they want done without you.

It's your job to provide appropriate interventions and to support the humans connected to the problems that disrupt efficiency and effectiveness in your organization. If nothing changes, you are letting your learners down. They are so desperate to be developed, they are willing to quit the company. Or worse, they are willing to stay and hamper the productivity of business by being unengaged. Your learners need you.

Is There Value in Being a Trusted Learning Advisor?

For far too long, we have limited our opportunities for organizational impact by following orders prescribed by someone who's not a skilled L&D practitioner. This behavior has fueled the idea that L&D is not intrinsically valuable to the business.

When you are a Trusted Learning Advisor, there is a transformational difference in the value the organization receives. Learners benefit from opportunities that inspire growth without being dragged down by ineffective learning. Departments benefit from increased engagement thanks to inspired learners, leading to more creativity and innovation. The business sees better productivity.

I know it. I believe it. But do you?

Although I have provided pages and pages of value that Trusted Learning Advisors *can* provide, it's you who must take a step back and reflect. Defining the value starts with reflecting on yourself and asking yourself if YOU believe the work matters, if YOU believe there is value. If you don't see your value, know how to define your value, and know how to communicate your value in a manner that your stakeholders will understand, chances are they won't know your value either.

ASK YOURSELF

What value do YOU provide:

- to the organization?
- to your stakeholder?
- to the business?
- to the learners?

As Trusted Learning Advisors, the opportunity for creating organizational value is plenty through both tangible and intangible benefits. As the connective tissue throughout the organization, you are a conduit creating equitable learning opportunities and optimizing learning initiatives to connect back to organizational strategies, all while providing developmental opportunities for the most important asset of any organization—the employees. Unfortunately, stakeholders are not inherently aware of the value you create, and you must face an ongoing challenge of skillfully and strategically overcoming their resistance toward your evolution as a Trusted Learning Advisor.

But when the stakeholders return and invite you to the table and listen, truly listen, and you move from an afterthought to a forethought, then you know you are on the path toward being a Trusted Learning Advisor. Being recognized as a Trusted Learning Advisor means your stakeholder recognizes the value that you bring.

As we move toward a future that embraces knowledge workers and drives toward innovation, we must redefine the role of L&D in developing and shaping organizational talent to meet the changing needs of the organization. It's time to find your place as a Trusted Learning Advisor, shaping organizational learning instead of just delivering training.

The real value of L&D within an organization is the ability to serve as the mechanism that aligns employee performance with organizational goals in an efficient and effective manner. We do more than create training; we identify skills gaps and create opportunities to fill them so that our organizations can continue to grow and do business competitively.

Remember this: **learning has the power to change lives.** Your learners are depending on you to be their advocates, to guide them in their development, and to help prepare them for the future. Your learners need you to be their support mechanism. Evolving into a Trusted Learning Advisor is the only way to secure your existence and ensure continued support for your learners.

You, the Trusted Learning Advisor, are the future of L&D.

Appendix I: Design Thinking

Design Thinking as a Problem-Solving Approach

With design thinking applications ranging from software development to urban planning, a design thinking approach lies at the root of some of our most successful products and platforms. The OXO products that make your life in the kitchen a little bit easier and cause you to wonder "Why didn't I think of that, it's so helpful!" resulted from design thinking. Apple attributes their innovative, user-friendly product design to design thinking. Oral B, Airbnb, and Uber Eats—all products of design thinking. But a lesser-known use case is that design thinking can be applied to problems with services and processes—such as Learning & Development (L&D). Many Trusted Learning Advisors have come to view design thinking as one of the most effective tactics in their problem-solving toolkits.

Design thinking is a five-phase set of principles for problem finding and creative problem solving—which is exactly our role as Trusted Advisors, finding problems and creatively solving them! Design thinking is a methodology that focuses on the end user, the learner, the customer, helping to pinpoint their needs and problems—even when they may not know what the problem is or are not able to articulate it clearly, much like what happens during the intake process with our stakeholders. Seeing the connection?

As someone who is viewed as a Trusted Learning Advisor, I appreciate being able to identify problems before my clients can even articulate them. I'm just paying attention to the things most others in the room are not. I've trained myself—like you can—to be good at problem finding and even better at problem solving. That's the essence of design thinking.

One of our main challenges as L&D professionals is that we typically don't know what business problems exist until a stakeholder points them out. That reactive approach must change.

As learning practitioners, we can borrow the concept of design thinking to become masterful at problem finding and problem solving. Too often our business partners order a deliverable in response to a time-sensitive event such as a product launch, a cohort of new hires who need to be trained, or an updated incentive program. Design thinking helps us be better business partners by providing a methodology to follow, evolving L&D from reactive order takers to proactive solution partners (aka Trusted Learning Advisors).

Different variations of design thinking models exist, but they're all based on the core concept of agility, creativity, and exploration. Design thinking is an approach to problem solving based on human-centered design practices that are easily applicable, flexible, nonlinear, and iterative, keeping all focus on the end user (learner). It's also a method that allows us to engage stakeholders in co-engineering a solution that maintains a keen focus on our shared priority—the learner.

I use the original five-stage model, also utilized by the Stanford d.school. The framework encourages curious and empathetic understanding while aiming to identify and prioritize uncovered opportunities. What sets design thinking apart from other problem-solving methodologies is that it starts with understanding the human, and only then seeks to define the problem statement. Design thinking puts the people first.

The following are the five steps in the design thinking model:

1 Empathize
2 Define
3 Ideate
4 Prototype
5 Test

Step 1. Empathize: Understanding Learners' Needs

Empathy and understanding are the foundation upon which all design thinking principles rest. Traditional problem-solving models often skip the step of understanding the problem from the end-user's perspective. Much like what we face during order taking, someone else decides what the problem is without actually engaging those facing the problem.

Rather than starting with defining a problem, design thinking starts with determining IF there is a problem by talking with those who may be impacted—empathizing with learners. Taking time to conduct qualitative research (aka interviews or empathy research) with employees, with no agenda other than to understand what they need and what challenges they face on their jobs, is essential. This process helps us take a step back and start with "problem finding" before moving into problem solving.

When we take orders from business partners without first doing the due diligence of understanding the problem, we potentially do a disservice to the business by wasting money and taking productive time away from employees for questionable training initiatives. We do an even bigger disservice to our learners by not providing the right remedy to solve their challenges.

Empathizing can mean advocating against a suggested deliverable from the business. A commitment to helping stakeholders save time and money means that we sometimes recommend against creating a deliverable when we don't believe it will boost the business or be useful to learners.

When we empathize with our learners, we meet them where they are—at their desks, working from home offices, on the sales floor, in warehouses or manufacturing plants. For example, these interviews may reveal that the best approach for teaching a new call center employee how to redirect a frustrated customer likely isn't web-based training with small print, bulleted lists, and an occasional static image.

A better method would allow these employees to observe an expert's diction and intonation, since they may not, for example, have the literacy skills to imagine a live conversation from onscreen text. The learner may be better served by a video and job aid with deescalating phrases and language in a legible font size that can be referenced immediately (aka performance support tools) and role-play opportunities.

The empathy phase of design thinking can help discern these distinctions. When we ignore learners' needs—or worse, simply bemoan the skills they lack—we set them up for failure.

Step 2. Define: Developing the Problem Statement

Compared with other methodologies, again, design thinking does not start with the problem statement—where most start. It starts with conducting research with people to uncover data, determining what the problem is rather than what our stakeholder has told us is the problem. It's very possible they are one and the same... but more often than not, they are not the same.

In the define phase, all the data captured is synthesized and analyzed to reveal users' needs and insights. This is also referred to as unpacking empathy findings, in order to scope a meaningful needs or problem statement and develop a point of view for the user. In true qualitative research manner, thematic analysis is used to identify the key findings and recurring themes from the interviews to develop the problem statement.

Tools such as user personas or "How might we...?" questions are used to help reframe the problem statement into a question to make it more meaningful and actionable and drive the design with the end-user in focus.

Step 3. Ideate: Brainstorming Solutions

The next step in design thinking is brainstorming solutions to address problem statements. Ideation is the "art of the possible." It is about identifying the broadest range of possibilities of solutions rather than just the one idea. Ideation goes broad and then narrows down in scope for solutions. A simple best practice during the ideation phase— the word "no" does not exist… only "yes," and the team builds on one another's ideas, no matter how crazy or audacious the idea might be.

Storyboarding, brainstorming, sketching, and mind mapping are examples of tools used to support the ideation phase. Creating constraints such as "How might we solve this problem with $1?" or "How might we solve this problem with $1,000,000?" helps to spur different ideas.

Once the ideas are captured, your team can vote on the ideas or plot them on a priority matrix to help identify the ideas to take forward to the next phase.

Step 4. Prototype: Create Representations

Prototyping means creating one or more quick representations of the ideas from the ideation phase. Prototypes can be one of two categories: low-fidelity and high-fidelity. In design thinking we tend to focus on low-fidelity prototypes—quick, low cost (or no cost), and minimal complexities to enable the end user to react to the idea and determine if it might solve the associated problem. This type of prototype is often referred to as an MVP—minimum viable product—meaning it offers just enough to give users something to react to and just enough functionality to provide feedback. Creating prototypes is a low-risk, quick way to test promising ideas under real-world conditions.

As a scaled-down version of the initiative, prototyping is a great and inexpensive way to partner with stakeholders as you continue designing and developing. This should save time and money as concerns are addressed early on, before the design is fully built out.

Step 5. Test: Expose Ideas and Gather User Feedback

The testing phase is the opportunity to capture feedback from users on their experience with the prototype. The data from testing will provide insight as to whether the perceived solution is heading in the right direction, or if further iteration is necessary. Testing provides the opportunity to actively observe how the user uses (or misuses) the prototype.

Testing prototypes and gathering feedback is key to continually improving L&D's products and services. Such an approach allows you to funnel more time and resources into ideas that gain traction, and reconsider those that show mediocre or poor results. The testing phase is an opportunity to capture data necessary to refine the prototype but also potentially to refine the point of view of the user.

CASE STUDY
Applying Design Thinking To Understanding Learner Experience

Problem—Is There Something Our Learners Need?

In 2017 when I started working with a large automobile manufacturer, I asked two questions: "How are we doing?", and "Could we be better?"

The answer to the first question was, "We are great. Our level 1 surveys are great. Learners like the trainers."

Okay. But could we be better? This was a question the team could not immediately answer. The team had their bias, preconceived assumptions, and limited data from the smile sheets (level 1 surveys), but the only way to really know if the learners needed something else was to find out from them directly. This was a perfect opportunity to utilize design thinking to better understand the needs of the learners.

Empathy Phase

The empathy phase involved spending several days preparing for learner qualitative interviews. To prepare, we brainstormed questions, created interview themes, refined questions after mock interviews, created the interview script and then ensured the team was comfortable with the questions and the anatomy of the interview process.

We then conducted 75 interviews across the United States. At the end of each interview day, we used design thinking and qualitative research tools, including an empathy map, four-box, and thematic analysis to begin to synthesize and analyze the information collected and define the problem statement.

Define Phase

Through our research and analysis we validated that the level 1 survey was correct—the learners did like the trainers. There was, however, something else we could be doing. The learners told us we were teaching them to be product experts, which is important, but we were missing a few key areas that would help improve their performance and engagement levels even more.

Learners said that:

- they wanted our help developing the skills necessary to actually sell the vehicles (aka soft or "power" skills), i.e. training in the arts of selling, negotiating and relationship building
- they needed inspiration and motivation to gain competency (LMS training was boring)
- they wanted training personalized based on their experiences and interests (new hires and veterans were receiving the same content)
- they wanted flexibility to learn what they wanted, but with enough structure to understand where they were going (we didn't explain the "why" clearly and dumped courses on their learning paths with no notice)
- they preferred hands-on and interactive learning so they could apply while they learned
- they recognized the need for learning, but felt time spent training was time away from selling

Stepping back to digest themes that emerged from the empathy interviews revealed to the L&D team a significant call to action: while our product training was receiving high marks, learners needed additional support in a variety of areas; problems we did not know existed.

Ideation Phase

During the ideation phase, we held a two-day brainstorming session that included learners, trainers, and people outside of L&D for diversity, and featured four steps:

1   idea sharing

2   sketching and storyboarding

3   voting

4   plotting on an impact and feasibility prioritization matrix

We divided into groups and sketched key ideas onto storyboards. Once finished, the groups reconvened to present their storyboard ideas. The full group then voted on the presentations: doable, wildcard (unknown if the idea is possible, but wanting to explore it regardless), or disruptive to the business.

The voting results were plotted against an impact and feasibility prioritization matrix with four categories: high risk/high reward; stars; quick hits; lower priority.

Realizing not every idea could be prototyped at once, we selected one idea within the "stars" category. The idea was in response to the problem: "How to provide training in the moment of need that doesn't take learners away from their jobs."

The idea involved creating a SMS/text-based system that acts as a digital mentor, using pull and push notifications that provide personalized training to employees by delivering answers to their questions, quizzing learners, and serving up relevant content as needed.

Prototype Phase

We reviewed existing technology in the marketplace and identified a chatbot to fulfill the requirements. The team then maximized our vendor-partner relationships to create a low-fidelity chatbot prototype within several days.

The prototype sought to identify where the learner population would adopt a chatbot as a training solution, whether chatbots were an effective technique to extend and reinforce learning, and what type of spacing intervals between chats worked best.

Test Phase

We were able to leverage an upcoming new automobile launch as the context for the prototype engagement. To ensure we identified a large enough test population, the team included learners from the initial empathy phase but also an employee population size totaling 2,000 users.

The design thinking team identified two prototype "test plans" for learners using the chatbots. Track A was a shorter time period (12 days) with daily chats. Track B was a longer time period (four weeks) with fewer chats (three per week.)

The team built a measurement plan that included measuring the chatbot opt-in rate, gauging an ongoing engagement rate, assessing pre- and post-quiz scores and a Net Promoter Score. While learners engaged with the chatbot during the prototype period, team members gathered feedback throughout the process from the trainers and learners on their experience.

At the conclusion of the testing phase, team members also captured feedback through surveys and individual discussions with learners. The feedback was very positive and provided enough data to encourage the team to move the solution into production after minor iterations.

Outcome

The design thinking initiative for us was a huge success. The team identified several needs for learners that we were not aware existed. Through the phases, we built relationships with learners, ensuring we stayed connected and seeking their continuous feedback.

The chatbot solution resulted in a major success for the team, indicated by its successful implementation, and became a recurring performance support tool utilized by the learner population.

The team ultimately integrated design thinking into our core strategy to ensure we were consistently staying connected with the learners through qualitative research to identify opportunities to solve problems for them, and support the idea of continuous improvement. Design thinking was the perfect methodology to utilize to support their evolution into Trusted Advisors. After all, design thinking is a focus on the people.

The question was: "Could we be better?", and the answer was: "Yes, we could."

Then again, I believe we can always be better.

Setting Expectations for Design Thinking

Design thinking is no silver bullet. It won't solve every performance problem and it's not a standalone framework for success. L&D also may need to meet other conditions to create value for stakeholders amid design thinking initiatives. For example, implementing design thinking may require corporate buy-in such as leadership support, openness, willingness to support and implement new ideas, and the trust and freedom to speak openly during the qualitative research process.

Although we like to believe we have all the answers, there is strength in inviting uncertainty into L&D by exploring ever-evolving learner needs. Design thinking helps us continually improve by creating a context in which we regularly disrupt our own established practices rather than being disrupted from the outside—part of the essence of being a Trusted Learning Advisor.

The next time one of your business partners self-diagnoses a performance problem and dictates a remedy for learners, consider applying a design thinking methodology. Making this recommendation will help you better serve the business, ensure the company's money is well invested, and guarantee you don't overlook the needs of your most important client: the learner.

Appendix II: Intake/Discovery Questions

The following are two sets of questions to ask your stakeholder to ensure you are conducting your due diligence. The first set is a list of proposed questions to proactively ask your stakeholder at the beginning of your relationship as well as on a periodic basis during the course of your relationship. The second set is a list of proposed questions to ask during your intake/discovery when a new order is received.

Questions to ask proactively throughout your relationship:

- What are your business priorities?
- What are the challenges you are facing?
- What are three key challenges your business is facing?
- What do the headwinds look like for the next three, six, or twelve months?
- How do you see your business shifting in the next four quarters?
- How is the industry shifting?
- What's the organizational culture like? What about the learning culture?
- Is learning an organizational strategy?
- What does innovation mean to you?
- What do you expect from Learning & Development (L&D) when they receive too many requests at the same time?
- For each line of business, are there business objectives that L&D has (or should have) an alignment to?

- What is the three- to five-year plan for the business unit and organization?
- What work is being done at the organizational level to identify critical priorities and areas of focus?
- How is change management addressed for major initiatives?
- How would your key stakeholders measure success? What pain points are you resolving for them?
- What's your opinion of your L&D function?
- What was your most memorable learning experience? Why?
- Who should I talk with to understand more about the business?
- Do you have any acronyms list, definition documents, or vocabulary decoders to help me understand and speak the language of the business?
- Do you have a mission, vision, and/or values statement for the business or organization?
- What feedback can you share with me to help make this partnership or project more successful?
- Tell me about a time where a learning initiative you were involved with did not meet your expectations.

Questions to ask when responding to the order:

- What's the problem you're trying to solve?
- How do you know this is a problem?
- Is this the first time this has been a problem? If not, what was done previously?
- Who are the people impacted? Who is the audience?
- Why this solution? Why now? Why not in six months? Or why not six months ago?
- Have you explored any other solutions?
- Has this solution previously been tried?
- Why is this important to you?
- Why do you think this will work?

- What is the operational metric(s) used to measure this?
- If you could predict the outcome, what would this look like?
- Who can I talk with to learn more about what it's like for them?
- How are you going to know that it's fixed when we're done?
- What behaviors are you trying to change? How is the behavior change being measured? What's the incentive for the learner to change? How will their manager support the training?
- What's going to have changed?
- How are you impacted by the project?
- What does success look like for this project?
- How does this intervention impact a critical business situation or relationship?
- Besides training, what other ways do you think this could be solved?
- What will happen if we don't do this training?
- What are the reasons why we shouldn't do this training?
- Who is the sponsor for this initiative to help ensure success?
- Who are your supporters? Change agents? Advocates? Master performers?
- How will the learners practice what they have learned? What does the practice look like in the context of their job?
- Is this just a "check the-box" activity that needs to be done, or can we measure success?
- What is the level of stake for the business: low, medium, or high?
- What are the project constraints?

Appendix III: Recommended Additional Reading

Author	Title	Theme
Clark Quinn	*Learning Science for Instructional Designers*	L&D
Clark Quinn	*Millennials, Goldfish, & Other Training Misconceptions*	L&D
Nigel Paine	*The Learning Challenge*	L&D
Nigel Paine	*Workplace Learning*	L&D
Nick Shackleton-Jones	*How People Learn*	L&D
Mirjam Neelen & Paul A. Kirschner	*Evidence Informed Learning Design*	L&D
Will Thalheimer	*Performance Focused Learner Surveys*	L&D
Peter Brown, Henry Roediger & Mark McDaniel	*Make it Stick: The science of successful learning*	L&D
Peter Block	*Flawless Consulting*	Consulting
David Maister, Charles Green & Robert Galford	*Trusted Advisor*	Consulting
Kevin R. Cope	*Seeing the Big Picture*	Org strategy

Author	Title	Theme
Morgan D. Jones	*The Thinker's Toolkit*	Problem solving
Shelle Rose Charvet	*Words That Change Minds*	Negotiation
Shawn Callahan	*Putting Stories to Work*	Storytelling
Nick Van Dam	*49 Tools for Learning & Development*	L&D
Nick Van Dam	*Elevating Learning & Development*	L&D
Julie Dirsken	*Design for How People Learn*	L&D
Cathy Moore	*Map it!*	L&D
Michael Allen	*Guide to e-Learning*	L&D
Mikeal Krogerus & Roman Tschappeler	*The Decision Book: Fifty models for strategic thinking*	Strategic thinking
Jeanne Liedtka	*Solving Problems with Design Thinking: Ten stories of what works*	Design thinking
Brandon Carson	*L&D's Playbook for the Digital Age*	L&D
Loren Sanders	*Empathy is Not a Weakness*	Empathy
Dan Pink	*To Sell is Human*	Selling/ Influence
Harry Beckwith	*Selling the Invisible*	Selling/ Influence

Appendix IV: You Might Be an Order Taker if...

Your stakeholder:

- makes all the decisions
- starts the conversation with: "I need you to create...," and you finish the conversation with: "Okay," and then you execute
- identifies a problem, determines the solution, tells you what to do, and you do it without conducting any due diligence
- says: "This is what the business wants, and you don't know the business"—and it's true that you don't know the business
- does not trust you

You:

- do not solve for the future, but only solve for today
- do not proactively spend time with your stakeholder, business, or learner to understand more about them
- are afraid to speak up to help your stakeholder identify alternative solutions, even ones that may not include training as the solution
- cannot identify three ways in which you provide value to your stakeholders
- think your role is to only put out fires (reactive)
- do not have relationships throughout the organization
- do not assert your educated and researched point of view
- do what your stakeholder wants, even if it's the wrong thing

- are creating learning solutions, but don't know how they tie back to organizational goals
- do not have a formalized, standardized intake process
- do not know learning sciences, learning methodologies, or learning frameworks
- have not asked for feedback from your stakeholder in the last 60 days
- do not conduct needs analysis, qualitative research, or root cause analysis before developing a learning solution
- do not have a relationship with your stakeholder
- do not have meaningful organizational relationships and do not understand the dependencies from one area to another

Appendix V: Trusted Learning Advisor Skills Inventory Matrix

Rate your proficiency in the following areas (place an X in the box that corresponds with your response)	Not Proficient	Slightly Proficient	Somewhat Proficient	Fairly Proficient	Completely Proficient
Communication Skills					
Public speaking (in person)					
Public speaking (virtual)					
Storytelling through presentation					
Setting expectations					
Interpersonal skills					
Training design and delivery					
Coaching or advising others					
Understanding verbal and non-verbal cues					
Interpersonal communication					
Influence					
Active listening					
Confidence/courage					
Feedback (giving and receiving)					
Connecting with learners/audience					
Collaboration and teamwork					
TOTAL					

75

L&D Practitioner Skills

Digital fluency

Learning technology tools (LMS, LXP, MOOC, chatbots, VR, AR, mixed reality, AI)

Human behavior and learning

Futures literacy

Instructional design

Project management

Evidence-based research

Measurement/data analysis

ADDIE Model

Ebbinghaus's Learning and Forgetting Curve

Human-centered design

Durable learning

ATD's Talent Capability Model

21st-century learning theories such as:

- andragogy and heutagogy
- transformative learning
- self-directed learning
- experiential learning
- project-based learning

Rate your proficiency in the following areas (place an X in the box that corresponds with your response)	Not Proficient	Slightly Proficient	Somewhat Proficient	Fairly Proficient	Completely Proficient
19th/20th-century learning theories such as:					
• behaviorism					
• cognitive					
• constructivism					
• humanism					
• connectivism					
TOTAL					115

Critical Thinking & Problem-Solving Skills

Conceptualization/visualization

Critical thinking

Open-mindedness

Learner experience (LX) design

User experience (UX) design

Problem evaluation and analysis

Agile thinking

Attention to detail

Design thinking

Proactivity

Growth mindset

Decision making

Continuous improvement—Lean/Six Sigma

Conflict resolution

TOTAL 70

Business Skills

Deep knowledge of the business

Awareness of organizational goals

Change management

Relationship building

Quantitative and qualitative data management

Consulting

Negotiation

Self-marketing and branding

Innovation

Strategic planning

TOTAL 50

Rate your proficiency in the following areas (place an X in the box that corresponds with your response)	Not Proficient	Slightly Proficient	Somewhat Proficient	Fairly Proficient	Completely Proficient
Human Skills					
Empathy					
Trustworthiness/honesty					
Leadership					
Self-awareness					
Emotional intelligence					
Flexibility/adaptability					
Learning/growth mindset					
Curiosity					
Creativity					
TOTAL					45
GRAND TOTAL					285

Points Rating Conventions

1- Not Proficient at All
2- Slightly Proficient
3- Somewhat Proficient
4- Fairly Proficient
5- Completely Proficient

Appendix VI: Partner Expectation & Commitment Charter

Success as a Trusted Learning Advisor is dependent on the relationship between you and your stakeholder. Your role in the partnership is to create an environment where you and your stakeholder can create value based on clear communication and understanding.

Completing the Partner Expectation & Commitment Charter helps to build trust and accountability as you are agreeing to be held to your commitments and expectations.

Instructions

Your Partner Expectation & Commitment Charter should explain your partnership. It should be written as if you are talking to one person. (Use "I" and "You" instead of "Stakeholder" and "L&D.") You will be presenting and discussing your charter to one stakeholder at a time.

The primary objective is to explain your expectations and commitment to your stakeholder, while also letting them know what they can expect from you in return.

Your stakeholder should also fill out the same charter. Filling out the charter can be done individually, meeting together afterwards to review, or it can be filled out together at the same time, using the questions as discussion points to gain immediate alignment.

Your Partner Expectation & Commitment Charter should be personal and authentic. It should sound like you, not like a leadership book or an HR manual.

The questions provided are a framework to guide your discussion, and are not meant to be an exhaustive list. Add to the questions as necessary.

PARTNER EXPECTATION & COMMITMENT CHARTER TEMPLATE

Date:

Name:

Stakeholder name:

Project:

How often charter will be reviewed:

Questions to discuss together to gain alignment and clarity:

- What is the preferred method, channel, and cadence of communication?
- How often will we meet?
- What matters most in this relationship?
- What's worked well in previous relationships?
- What should be done differently this time?
- How do you define and measure the success of this relationship?
- How do you prefer to handle conflict?
- How will we work together when something goes sideways or is not working in the way we expected?
- What can I expect of you?
- What commitments can you make to me?
- What should I know about you and the way you work?

- How do you define success?
- What does innovation mean to you?
- How do you prioritize and determine what is most important to the business?

The output of these questions will help you and your stakeholder articulate what you expect to receive as a partner, but also what you expect to be giving, including insights that would be valuable for how you work together and how you communicate.

It's an opportunity for you to share what is important to you, and what your stakeholder should know about you to set you both up for success.

INDEX

EU Representative (GPSR)

Authorised Rep Compliance Ltd, Ground Floor, 71 Lower Baggot Street, Dublin, D02 P593, Ireland

www.arccompliance.com

www.ingramcontent.com/pod-product-compliance
Lightning Source LLC
Jackson TN
JSHW060902210225
79385JS00018B/264